HIGH
COLD WAR

HIGH
COLD WAR

Strategic Air Reconnaissance
and the Electronic Intelligence War

Robert Jackson

Patrick Stephens Limited

© Robert Jackson 1998

First published in 1998

British Library Cataloguing-in-Publication Data:
A catalogue record for this book
is available from the British Library

ISBN 1 85260 584 7

Library of Congress catalog card No. 97-77760

Patrick Stephens Limited is an imprint of
Haynes Publishing, Sparkford,
Nr Yeovil, Somerset, BA22 7JJ

Tel. 01963 440635 Fax: 01963 440001
Int. tel: +44 1963 440635 Fax: +44 1963 440001

E-mail: sales@haynes-manuals.co.uk
Web site: http://www.haynes.com

Haynes North America Inc.,
861 Lawrence Drive, Newbury Park,
California 91320 USA

Typeset by J. H. Haynes & Co. Ltd, Sparkford

Printed in Hong Kong

Contents

Introduction

ON THE MORNING of 2 September 1958, a four-engined Lockheed C-130 Hercules of the United States Air Force took off from the NATO air base at Incirlik, in southern Turkey, and set course northwestwards. The Hercules was attached to the 7406th Combat Support Squadron, which was normally based at Rhein-Main Air Base near Frankfurt, Germany.

The Hercules, which had first entered service with the USAF's Military Air Transport Service in December 1956, was an amazingly versatile aircraft, able to carry a wide variety of cargoes and to operate, if necessary, out of rough airstrips anywhere in the world. It was still to be the workhorse of America's air transport fleet, and the principal tactical transport aircraft of many other nations, 40 years later.

On that September day, however, the C-130 cruising over the mountains of Turkey was not one of the USAF's transport fleet. It was an EC-130 operated by the US National Security Agency, and it was on a signals intelligence gathering mission. Its spacious fuselage was packed with advanced electronic equipment and it carried a crew of 17 men, 13 of whom were radio and radar specialists. Their mission was to intercept and identify signals from the network of Soviet radar stations to the north of the Black Sea and in Armenia and Georgia; signals that would tell them not only what type of radar was being used, but also reveal its range and other information.

The first leg of the EC-130's flight took it high over the 12,000 ft peaks of the Canik mountains. Ninety minutes and 350 miles out from Incirlik the aircraft was over Trabzon, on the north coast of Turkey and the pilot, Captain Paul E. Duncan, turned right through 90 degrees and headed for Lake Van, 250 miles away in the south-east corner of Turkey. This new heading took the Hercules parallel with the border of Soviet Armenia, which was about 100 miles away off the aircraft's port beam.

The Hercules never reached Lake Van, and an extensive search for it all over eastern Turkey turned up no clues as to its fate. On 6 September, after considerable discussion, the American Embassies in Moscow and Tehran formally asked the Russians and Iranians if the aircraft had come down in their territory, having strayed over the border by accident; both governments denied all knowledge of it.

Then, on 12 September, the Soviet Foreign Ministry stated that the wreckage of an American military aircraft had been discovered near the village of Sassnaken in Soviet Armenia, some 35 miles north of the town of Yerevan, and that six badly mutilated bodies had been recovered. The Russians claimed that the EC-130 had deliberately violated their air space, an allegation which – in view of the circumstances surrounding

The ubiquitous Lockheed C-130 Hercules provided an ideal platform for electronic intelligence operations.

the EC-130's mission – the Americans naturally denied. The next day, in fact, the American charge d'affaires in Moscow handed a note to the Soviet Foreign Ministry, alleging that the Hercules had been intercepted by Soviet fighters close to the Turkish–Armenian border, that the American pilot had obeyed the fighters' instructions to follow them eastwards, but that his aircraft had been deliberately destroyed shortly afterwards. It was claimed that eye-witnesses on the Turkish side of the border had seen the Hercules turn towards the east; soon afterwards, they had heard an explosion and had seen a column of smoke rising from a point within Soviet territory. These allegations were flatly denied by the Russians.

Then the Americans played their trump card. Monitoring stations in Turkey, they stated, had made a tape recording from a Soviet radio frequency of what appeared to be R/T chatter between four Russian pilots. The date and time of the transmission tallied exactly with that of the EC-130's disappearance, and the translated text of the Russians' conversation, as released by the USAF, was as follows:

'I see the target, to the right'
'I see the target.'
'Roger.'
'The target is a big one.'
'Attack by...' (transmission garbled)
'Roger.'
'The target is a four-engined transport.'
'Target speed is three-zero-zero. I am going along with it. It is turning towards the fence.'

At this point the transmission became garbled, the voices of the Russian pilots high-pitched and excited. Then:

'The target is burning.'
'There's a hit.'
'The target is burning, 582.'
'281, are you attacking?'
'Yes, yes, I...' (transmission garbled).
'The target is burning...the tail assembly is falling off the target. 582, can you see me? I am in front of the target.'
'Look, look at him, he will not get away, he is already going down.'
'Yes, he is going down. I will finish him off, boys, I will finish him off on this run.'
'The target has lost control. It is going down.'
'The target has turned over...aha, you see, it is falling!'
'All right, form up, head for home.'
'The target started burning after my third pass...'

The Americans made no admission that the Hercules had penetrated Soviet air space, but there was no longer any doubt that this had happened when, on 24 September, the Russians – who had dismissed the tape recording as a crude fabrication – returned the remains of six crew members, only four of whom could be identified. No other bodies were handed over, despite repeated American requests. The US Deputy Under-Secretary of State, Robert Murphy, subsequently issued a statement to the effect that 'the American pilot, as a result of signals transmitted by radio beacons in Soviet Georgia and Armenia, had probably made a navigational error which resulted in his unintentionally crossing the Soviet border.' The statement then went on to claim that the Hercules had then been fired on by Soviet aircraft and destroyed.

In fact, the statement implied that the EC-130 had been deliberately lured over the Soviet border by false radio signals and then shot down. If Captain Paul Duncan had been relying on his radio aids rather than on visual navigation – which was likely, since significant landmarks in the rugged terrain of northeast Turkey were few, and in any case the C-130 was over cloud during the last leg of its flight – then the Russians could have jammed the Lake Van radio beacon transmissions and superimposed their own. A few degrees' deviation from its planned course would have been enough to take the Hercules over Soviet territory. It is likely that Captain Duncan only realised his mistake when the Russian fighters appeared, and that he immediately turned west towards the frontier; but by then it was too late.

Then, in October 1958, came another extraordinary twist to what was already a bizarre story. *Sovietskaya Aviatsiya*, the daily newspaper of the Soviet Air Force, published an article purporting to describe an 'air exercise' in which four Soviet jet fighters shot down an 'intruding enemy aircraft'. Significantly, the callsigns of two of the fighters mentioned in the article were identical with those on the American tape; courses and altitudes were also similar. According to the article, the four fighters were scrambled from separate airfields with an interval of several minutes between each pair and were guided to the target by two fighter controllers, Major Kulikov and Captain Romanyuta. The callsigns of the leading fighters (which were unidentified, but probably MiG-17s) were 582 and 281. They were flown by Lieutenants Lopatkov and

Gavrilov. The article stated that by the time the second pair of fighters arrived on the scene, their take-off having been delayed by a sandstorm, Lopatkov and Gavrilov had already made three passes at the target and set it on fire. The work of destruction was completed by the other two pilots, Lieutenants Kucheryayev and Ivanov.

For years afterwards, there was speculation that some of the American crew members had survived and had been interrogated and then imprisoned by the Russians, but in 1995, following the end of the Cold War, the incident was investigated by a joint US-Russian commission, which investigated the crash site and interviewed witnesses. An excavation turned up human bone fragments at the scene, and no evidence was produced to suggest that there had been any survivors.

As to the theory that the Hercules had been deliberately lured over the border, this remained a possibility; just a few weeks earlier, on 27 June 1958, a USAF C-118 transport had crashed inside Soviet territory in the same area. Radio deception techniques were by no means new, and they could be effective; during the Second World War, in Britain, the Radio Branch of the Post Office Engineering Department had devised masking beacons – known as Meacons – which were designed to interfere with the Luftwaffe's navigational aids. On the night of 6/7 July 1941, to give just one example, Meacon jamming of the Luftwaffe's navigational beacon at Noordwijk in Holland caused the crews of three *Kustenfliegergruppe* 106, operating off the north-east coast of England to become disorientated; all three aircraft flew into high ground near Bridlington.

The story of the Hercules shootdown of September 1958 is well known. At the time, it generated much publicity in the world's press. And that is the point; it was the first time that a covert intelligence-gathering mission (although it was not admitted as such for years afterwards) had received major media coverage.

For the first time, the general public began to have an inkling that a secret war was being fought; a war of cat and mouse between east and west that involved aerial spying on a routine basis.

What the public did not know was that this campaign of aerial espionage had been in progress almost since the end of the Second World War, and that it had already claimed dozens of lives.

1

Early Secret Overflights

AIR RECONNAISSANCE IS almost as old as man's attempts to fly. Chinese man-lifting kites, as described by the Venetian explorer Marco Polo in the 14th century, may have been used for military observation purposes, although there is no firm evidence; but in 1794 the Army of the French Republic used observation balloons in its campaign against the Austrians, and balloons were employed by various nations during the conflicts of the 19th century, most notably in the American Civil War.

The First World War brought a new dimension to air reconnaissance: aerial photography. The technique was pioneered before the outbreak of hostilities by No. 3 Squadron of the Royal Flying Corps under Captain H. R. M. Brooke-Popham. Because of a lack of funding the officers had to buy their own cameras and adapt them for aerial work by trial and error, but they nevertheless validated the concept; in 1914 they succeeded in producing a complete set of photographs covering the defences of the Isle of Wight and the Solent.

The original cameras were of the folding type with bellows and loaded with plates. They were cumbersome to handle in the air, especially in cold weather, and produced poor results. In the autumn of 1914 Major W. G. H. Salmond made a study of the French photographic organisation, which at that time was more advanced than any other, and as a result the RFC formed an experimental photographic section staffed by Lieutenants J. T. C. Moore-Brabazon and C. D. M. Campbell, Sergeant F. C. V. Laws and Second Air Mechanic W. D. Corse. These four men set about designing a new, effective air camera and completed their task in less than two months. While they were doing so, the first successful photographic reconnaissance was carried out in January 1915, when pictures were taken of some brick stacks south of the La Bassée Canal. These revealed a new German trench and contributed greatly to the success of the Allied attack that went in on 6 January. From then on, aerial photography was to be a vital factor in operations on all fronts; its importance was such that the need to protect photographic reconnaissance aircraft brought about the need for fighter escorts, which in turn gave enormous impetus to the development of air fighting as a whole.

On the Western Front, air photography was directed in the main towards trench registration, which in practice meant flying over the enemy's trench systems and taking photographs so that interpreters could log any changes in the defences. This was tactical reconnaissance in support of the Army; the only long-range strategic reconnaissance missions of the First World War were carried out by the German Navy's

Zeppelin and the Army's Schütte-Lanz airships, the former scouting on behalf of the High Seas Fleet and the latter on the Eastern Front.

Air reconnaissance and the interrogation of prisoners were the two primary sources of intelligence during the 1914–18 war. After 1918 the picture changed, and the most important information on the activities of potentially hostile nations came via diplomatic channels. The development of photographic reconnaissance stagnated – although the Royal Air Force used it extensively in mapping areas such as Iraq and the North-West Frontier of India – and despite promising experiments, notably in the United States, PR remained a backwater.

Germany was a notable exception. Not long before the outbreak of the Second World War, Generaloberst Freiherr Werner von Fritsch, an officer of the old school and a former cavalryman, who was Commander-in-Chief of the German Army during the early years of the Nazi regime, let fall a prophetic remark. 'The next war,' he said, 'will be won by the military organisation with the most effective photographic reconnaissance.'

In 1938–9 it seemed that the Germans had a clear lead in the field. They had better scientific instruments, they had better cameras fitted with those splendid Zeiss lenses, and they had a very promising photographic aircraft in the Heinkel He 119, a highly streamlined design that was one of the fastest aircraft produced by the German aviation industry before the war. In the event, the He 119 never went into production for the Luftwaffe, and at the outbreak of war the German strategic PR task was undertaken by the Dornier Do 17 and, later, by versions of the Junkers Ju 86 and Ju 88.

During the 1930s, the Germans paid far more attention to the development of strategic photographic reconnaissance than did either the British or the French, and put their theories to the test in the Spanish Civil War with aircraft like the Do 17 and the Heinkel He 70, an adaptation of a fast mail-carrier. German developments, however, had not gone unnoticed in Britain, and the basic initiative for change came from Wing Commander F. W. Winterbotham, Chief of Air Intelligence in the Secret Intelligence Service. Winterbotham had been receiving the photographic results of some clandestine French flights made over German territory in the late 1920s and early 1930s, and he began looking around for someone to undertake similar work on behalf of the British Government. The expansion of the newly-created Luftwaffe was giving much cause for concern; although from 1935 there was signals intelligence on the German Air Force, it was mostly available in the form of W/T traffic from heavier aircraft, as short-range HF/VHF voice transmissions from fighter units and so on could not be received in the UK, and some photographic coverage was necessary to provide a more comprehensive picture of the Luftwaffe's strength and dispositions.

Winterbotham was steered towards a very remarkable man called Sidney Cotton, once described rather aptly as a 'buccaneering entrepreneur', who agreed to undertake a series of clandestine photographic missions over Germany for the British and French intelligence services, who were co-operating closely at the time. The aircraft selected by Cotton for the purpose was the Lockheed 12A, two of which were purchased with funds provided jointly by the UK and French governments. The purchase was concluded in September 1938, with Imperial Airways acting as an agent, and one aircraft – painted pale green overall – was positioned at Heston in Middlesex in November. To maintain secrecy, the aircraft was registered under a company called the Aeronautical Sales and Research Corporation.

The beautifully streamlined Heinkel He 70 fast mailplane was used in the reconnaissance role in the Spanish Civil War.

A Lockheed Electra, similar to the one used by Sidney Cotton on his clandestine photo-reconnaissance missions over Germany.

The first sortie was flown on 10 March 1939, when Mannheim was photographed. In the event of the Lockheed being intercepted by German fighters, its installation of three cameras could be jettisoned through a hole in the cabin floor. A Leica camera, concealed behind a sliding panel, was also installed in each wing leading edge; Cotton planned to use these for low-level photography. During the months that followed he ranged far and wide over Germany, usually taking his photographs from 20,000 feet, and also went to Malta, from which island base he photographed Italian naval installations.

Meanwhile, the embryo photographic reconnaissance organisation at Heston had begun to expand. In the course of 1939 Cotton was joined by Squadron Leader A. Earle (photographic officer), Flight Lieutenant R. H. Niven (a Canadian on a short service commission in the RAF, who was well known to Cotton), Flying Officer H. Blyth (liaison officer), Pilot Officer H. G. Belcher (equipment officer) and Flying Officer M. V. Longbottom. Maurice Longbottom, predictably known as 'Shorty', joined the organisation for flying duties; Cotton had met him in Malta during one of his visits and enlisted him as an assistant, not without having to overcome a few administrative problems with the AOC Malta. Eighteen other ranks were also posted to Heston.

In August 1939, as a result of working with the dynamic and determined Cotton, Longbottom produced a memorandum entitled *Photographic Reconnaissance in Enemy Territory in War*, which he submitted to the Air Ministry. It divided reconnaissance into two categories: tactical work in the immediate vicinity of the front line and strategic reconnaissance of enemy territory behind the zone of conflict. What was remarkable about the document was the way in which Longbottom foresaw the problems of reconnaissance – more dangerous than bombing, in his opinion – and suggested the solution. In his words: 'This type of reconnaissance (strategic) must be done in such a manner as to avoid the enemy fighter and aerial defences as completely

The Lockheed XC-35, a modified Electra developed secretly by Lockheed in 1937, was the first aircraft with a pressurised cabin to fly in the sub-stratosphere.

as possible. The best method of doing this appears to be the use of a single small machine relying solely on its speed, climb and ceiling to avoid detection.' What Longbottom was in effect advocating was a small, stealthy aircraft, relying on speed and altitude for its survival, rather than on any ability to fight its way out of trouble.

Between 26 July and the end of August 1939 the Lockheed made a number of trips to Berlin, landing at the capital and, of course, photographing installations en route. John Weaver, one of the earliest members of what was to become the Photographic Reconnaissance Unit, flew with Cotton several times and recalls that, 'On one occasion he (Cotton) flew over to Tempelhof, and Goering and his lieutenants were there. Seeing the aircraft, they made a number of enquiries as to whom it belonged. On finding out, they approached Cotton for a flight and asked where he would take them. Cotton was a very clever chap and said, 'I have a dear old aunt who lives in such an area, and if you have no objections we could fly over there.' It was agreed and off they set, but what they didn't know was that dear old Sidney was pressing the tit the whole time, taking photographs.'

Cotton's last clandestine flight before the outbreak of war was in the afternoon of 2 September 1939 when, at the request of the Admiralty, he carried out a reconnaissance of the Elbe estuary where units of the German fleet were at anchor. The action did not endear Cotton to the Air Ministry, who knew nothing about the mission until after it had taken place; nevertheless, valuable photographs of the German Fleet's dispositions were in the hands of the Director of Naval Intelligence that same evening.

Germany's mighty Graf Zeppelin *commercial airship was said to have been used for clandestine reconnaissance missions during the inter-war years.*

On the outbreak of war Heston airfield was requisitioned by the RAF, becoming a satellite of Northolt under No. 11 Group, Fighter Command, and the Heston Flight – as the PR organisation was now known, with Sidney Cotton in charge of it as an acting wing commander – also came under Fighter Command. The Flight actually came into existence officially on 22 September 1939, when it was authorised to act as a strategic reconnaissance unit on behalf of the RAF.

The activities of the RAF's photographic reconnaissance organisation – eventually expanded to a force of several squadrons operating in all theatres and equipped with Spitfires and Mosquitos – took place under war conditions and are therefore outside the scope of this book, the theme of which is clandestine operations in peacetime.

Returning to operations of this kind, the Germans carried out a series of overflights of targets in eastern Europe – Poland, Czechoslovakia and, later, the Soviet Union – prior to the outbreak of hostilities. Overflights of Poland and Czechoslovakia were made by reconnaissance variants of the Dornier Do 17 and Heinkel He 111 belonging to the *Aufklarungsgruppe* – Reconnaissance Group – of the German Army High Command, joined later by the high-altitude Junkers Ju 86P. In the spring and early summer of 1941 this unit, under the command of Oberstleutnant Theodor Rowehl, carried out many high-altitude sorties over the western Soviet Union, gathering valuable photographic intelligence of Russian airfields in preparation for the planned German invasion. There is little doubt that civil aircraft belonging to the German airline Lufthansa also took clandestine reconnaissance photographs of British targets – although strangely enough there is no firm evidence of this – and the German commercial airship *Graf Zeppelin* is said to have secretly photographed the whole of Britain's south-east coast, furnishing Luftwaffe Intelligence with much information on the new radar stations that were to play such a vital part in the Battle of Britain a few years later.

However, it was the Japanese – whose military prowess and ingenuity had for so long been ignored in the western world – who were among the first to recognise the need for effective long-range air reconnaissance and to exploit it in peacetime by means of clandestine missions. In the early 1930s the Mitsubishi aircraft company designed an experimental land-based attack bomber known as the Hiro G2H1, of which they built eight prototypes. Although the G2H1 was seriously underpowered it was of modern configuration, employing several design features incorporated by contemporary Junkers aircraft, and development of the basic design led to the 8-Shi long-range reconnaissance monoplane which, flying for the first time in April 1934, was one of the first Japanese aircraft to employ a retractable undercarriage.

For its day, the performance of the 8-Shi (also known by the manufacturer's designation Ka-9) was impressive. It could outstrip most contemporary Japanese fighters; it had a normal range of 2,700 miles and, with extra fuel tanks, this could be increased to over 3,700 miles. Despite these qualities, development of the 8-Shi was abandoned, but the experience gained in its design was put to good use in the development of an attack bomber, the Mitsubishi Type 96 G3M1.

The prototype G3M1, powered initially by two Hiro Type 91 water-cooled engines, made its first flight in July 1935 and reached a maximum speed of slightly over 195 mph at 5,000 feet. Later aircraft were fitted with 1,000 hp Kinsei 45 radial engines, boosting the maximum speed by 40 mph, and it was this variant – the G3M2, later to be given the code-name *Nell* by the Allies in the Pacific War – that entered quantity production.

On 14 August 1937, 18 G3M2s took off from the Japanese Naval Air Base at Taipei, Formosa, to deliver long-range attacks on the Chinese cities of Hangkow and Kwangteh. The next day, more bombers of the same type flew from Kyushu in the Japanese Home Islands to bomb Shanghai and Nanking. At that time it was the longest strategic bombing mission undertaken by any aircraft.

The G3M2 was used extensively in the long-range reconnaissance role during the Sino–Japanese conflict, and the operational experience gained in this field by Japanese Navy crews was to prove invaluable to Japan's military planners in 1940 and early 1941 as they worked out their strategy for the coming offensive in the Pacific. Although the concentration of the US Pacific Fleet on Pearl Harbor in the autumn of 1940 was no secret, there were still serious gaps in Japanese intelligence on other major American bases in the Pacific, and although a constant flow of intelligence material reached Tokyo from Japanese agents in the Pacific islands, much of it was worthless without firm corroboration.

Air reconnaissance was the obvious answer, since most of the US bases the Japanese wished to photograph lay well within the range of the Navy's G3M2s. Nevertheless, since Japan would not be ready to strike in the Pacific for some months, any such operations would have to be carried out under strict secrecy to avoid aggravating the already tense situation in the Pacific area. The main problem was that Japanese Intelligence required a whole series of reconnaissance flights which increased the risk of the aircraft being detected, and although the Japanese Navy could pass off an occasional aircraft found wandering over an American base as a stray lost on a navigation exercise, they could not do so repeatedly.

Any risk involved, however, was held to be fully justified, and in late March 1941 the 3rd Air Corps, Imperial Japanese Navy, was specially formed to carry out the clandestine reconnaissance missions on the orders of Admiral Isoroku Yamamoto, the brilliant naval commander who was to be responsible for many of Japan's early successes in the Pacific War. The 3rd Air Corps was based at the Takao Naval Air Base on Formosa, and its first G3M2s were ferried out from Japan on 1 April. The aircraft were painted light grey overall and carried no national markings. Although standard production machines, the G3M2s were stripped of all defensive armament, which permitted a substantial increase in altitude performance, and a single camera was mounted in the cockpit on a special attachment that enabled it to be swung outboard for vertical shots.

Intensive training began with the arrival of the first aircraft, the crews – all veterans of the Sino–Japanese campaign – pushing the G3M2s to the limit of their endurance and photographing a wide variety of simulated targets over a great arc stretching from the Pacific to the South China Sea. At this stage the crews did not know the true nature of their mission, although the fact that their aircraft bore no insignia and that the 3rd Air Corps was kept strictly apart from the other units at Takao gave rise to much speculation.

By 15 April 1941 the Air Corps was up to full strength, with three squadrons of twelve aircraft each. The following day, the crews were assembled and were at last told the nature of their mission. It was emphasised that everything possible had to be done to avoid interception by American fighters; at the heights the G3M2s were to fly, anti-aircraft fire should present no problem, and even if the Americans did detect the Japanese aircraft and sent up fighters the G3M2s should be well clear of the target area by the time the interceptors had climbed to altitude. If a G3M2 was forced down in hostile territory, its crew were to take all possible steps to ensure the complete destruction of their machine. As a final last minute measure, the 7.7 mm guns were replaced in the 3rd Air Corps' aircraft and the crews were permitted to defend themselves in the event of attack by US fighters; in the eyes of the Intelligence Staff in Tokyo, the importance of getting the all-important photographs back to base outweighed the risk of provoking a major international incident.

The 3rd Air Corps' first operational mission was flown on 18 April 1941. It involved a 1,300-mile round trip from Takao to Legaspi on the island of Luzon, in the Philippines, to photograph harbour installations, a military airfield and a barracks. The weather was perfect, with scattered cirrus cloud at about 25,000 feet and a flight visibility of 50 miles. The G3M2, piloted by Lieutenant Sudo, climbed to 11,000 feet and maintained that altitude until Luzon was sighted. Keeping at least 15 miles to the east of the island Sudo climbed to 25,000 feet, crossing Catanduances Island on a southerly heading. In front of the aircraft lay Mount Mayon, the landmark that dominated Legaspi.

Sudo took the G3M2 up to 28,000 feet and began his run-in, a crew member standing by to operate the camera. A blast of freezing air roared into the cockpit through the open camera hatch; the outside air temperature was minus 20°C and the crew were numb with cold despite their heavy flying clothing. As the aircraft passed over Legaspi its camera took a photograph every 15 seconds. Sudo turned through 180 degrees, making a second run over the objective before heading eastwards towards the open sea. Three hours later the G3M2 touched down at Takao at the end of a faultless mission, having secured 36 excellent photographs of the Legaspi area.

Five days later, 21 G3M2s took off from Takao for a new location on Peleliu in the Palau Islands, 1,400 miles away, preceded by a ship carrying ground crews and equipment. Only 300 miles from Formosa the aircraft, flying in formation, ran into dense cloud and became split up. Fourteen returned to Takao; the remainder struggled on and landed on Peleliu after a flight of more than ten hours. They were joined by the others a week later, following several days of high winds and torrential rain which swept the Pacific.

Operating from Peleliu the aircraft of the 3rd Air Corps photographed objectives on Mindanao, in the southern Philippines, Jolo Island, and northern New Guinea. Flights of up to twelve hours were routine, the photographic runs over the target usually being made at 28,000 feet. Many of the missions involved photographing airfields, which would later be used by the Japanese in their early successful offensive in the Pacific.

In May 1941 the bulk of the 3rd Air Corps moved to the island of Truk in the Caroline Islands, from where sorties were flown over Rabaul and other island targets in the area. The following month one flight of G3M2s was transferred to Tinian in the Marianas to undertake what was potentially the most dangerous mission so far: a photographic survey of US installations on Guam, one of America's main Pacific bases in the same island group. Since the distance from Tinian to Guam was a little over 100 miles, the G3M2s had to climb fast and were stripped down to achieve the maximum possible altitude, in some cases over 30,000 feet. The whole of the island was successfully photographed in three sorties, but this time the presence of the Japanese aircraft had not gone unnoticed. On 20 June, 1941, the Japanese Government received a strongly-worded note from the United States, protesting at what appeared to be illegal flights of an unspecified nature by Japanese military aircraft over US territory. The Japanese naturally denied everything, but it was clear that further clandestine missions would be too dangerous, and in any case the activities of the 3rd Air Corps had provided Japanese Intelligence with at least 90 per cent of the information it required.

The secret flights were consequently discontinued, and shortly afterwards the 3rd Air Corps was transferred to Hainan Island. From there, it took part in the Japanese invasion of southern French Indo-China, operating in the conventional bombing role. At the end of the Indo-China campaign the 3rd Air Corps returned to Kanoya Naval Air Station in Japan, where it disbanded. The crews were scattered among other naval air units, and few of them survived the war.

Their missions, long overlooked by historians, deserve to be remembered. They were the true precursors of the clandestine intelligence-gathering missions that would be flown a decade and more later under vastly different and infinitely more dangerous circumstances, as the superpowers that dominated the post-war world faced one another in armed confrontation.

2

The Countermeasures War, 1939–45

On the night of 14/15 November 1940, 450 German bombers attacked the city of Coventry, designated by Luftwaffe Intelligence as an important munitions centre and therefore a legitimate military target. They dropped 500 tons of high explosive and 30 tons of incendiary bombs into the heart of the city, razing it to the ground.

The main force was guided to the target by two squadrons of Heinkel He 111H-3s of KG100, following a radio beam sent out by a *Knickebein* transmitter on the French coast. A steady signal in the pilot's headphones meant that he was on course; dots or dashes meant that he was straying to left or right. Each bomber was equipped with a special radio receiver known simply as 'X-Apparatus'. A signal, automatically triggered by a second beam cutting across the first at an angle from another *Knickebein* station, indicated that the bombers were now ten miles from the target. As soon as this signal was received, each radio operator pressed a switch, starting up a clock on his instrument panel. Five miles further on, in response to a signal from a third beam, the radio operator pressed the switch again, stopping the first pointer and starting a second. It was now up to the pilot to hold the bomber steady on the final run-in to the target. Apart from opening the bomb doors, that was all he had to do; everything else was automatic. When the second pointer on the radio operator's clock became superimposed on the first, it triggered the electrical bomb release.

Night after night during the winter of 1940–41, London, the Midlands, Merseyside, Wales, Tyneside, Plymouth, Exeter, Southampton, Bristol and many other places were subjected to beam-guided attacks led by KG100 and another pathfinder unit, III/KG28, the Heinkels ranging as far afield as Belfast. It was the beginning of a radio countermeasures war that merits an examination in detail, for the technology it produced was to have enormous significance in post-war strategic air intelligence operations.

British Intelligence had been aware for some months that the Germans were developing radio beams as aids to navigation and bombing. As early as June 1940 Professor Lindemann, the scientific adviser to the British War Cabinet, had reported to Winston Churchill that the Germans had developed a radio beam by means of which they would be able to bomb by day or night, whatever the weather. On 21 June the Prime Minister convened an emergency meeting which was attended by senior RAF officers, scientists and the Deputy Director of Scientific Research at the Air Ministry, Dr (later Professor) R. V. Jones. The latter informed the meeting that for some months hints had been coming in from all sorts of sources on the Continent indicating that the Germans had some novel form of night bombing technique on which they pinned great hopes. In some way it seemed to be linked with the code name *Knickebein* (Crooked Leg), which British Intelligence had come across several times without being able to explain. (In fact, the primary sources of intelligence were the RAF's 'Y' Service, which monitored enemy transmissions, and *Ultra*, the high-grade intelligence output from the Code and Cipher Establishment at Bletchley Park, whose activities were to remain a well-kept secret for 30 years.)

The first theory was that enemy agents had somehow managed to plant radio homing beacons in and around major British targets, but this idea was soon dismissed. Then RAF reconnaissance aircraft photographed three curiously-shaped towers on the German-occupied coast, structures which did not seem to be the right shape for any known type of radio or radar transmitter. Soon afterwards, a German bomber was shot down near Liverpool, and an examination of the wreck revealed that the aircraft carried radio equipment whose elaborate nature suggested that it was connected with something other than the ordinary *Lorenz* blind landing system.

From an analysis of this equipment, together with statements made by German aircrew who broke down under interrogation, Intelligence deduced that the Germans might be planning to navigate and bomb on some sort of radio beam system. At first the idea was greeted with some incredulity, particularly on the part of senior officers of RAF Bomber Command, whose own crews relied entirely on visual navigation and bombing. Above 20,000 feet, they argued, the stars were nearly always visible, which meant that with thorough training in astro-navigation the bomber crews should be able to find the way to their targets without too much difficulty. What the RAF commanders did not realise at this stage was that only a very small percentage of RAF Bomber Command's crews were accurately locating the target. It would be months before these inaccuracies were fully appreciated and the RAF gave priority to the development of its own radio navigation systems.

Nevertheless, once the British scientists had divined the true purpose of the *Knickebein* transmitters it did not take the scientists long to devise effective countermeasures against them. On Churchill's orders, priority was given to the erection of radio transmitters on the coast of southern England for the purpose of jamming the enemy beams. The general principle behind the jamming operations was that the countermeasures equipment strengthened the signal from one half of the split beam and not from the other, which meant that an enemy pilot trying to fly so that the signals from both halves of the split beam were balanced would go badly off course.

The first British countermeasures transmitters were operational by the middle of August 1940, their targets being the two *Ruffian* stations – as the RAF code-named the *Knickebein* transmitters – near Dieppe and Cherbourg. It was not long before the Germans realised that attempts were being made to jam their stations, and they in turn implemented counter-countermeasures. During September 1940 they installed X-Apparatus, together with new ground and airborne equipment which worked in a different frequency range. By the middle of September the British had learned enough about the new equipment to devise more countermeasures, but the necessary jamming equipment could not be produced for another two months, which meant that the Heinkels of KG100 could carry out their pathfinding operations without interference.

During the last days of October, British Intelligence received indications that the enemy would undertake a large raid with the help of the new equipment before the middle of November, and the assessment was that the target would be either London or Liverpool. This assessment, however, was tragically wrong: the objective of the German experiment was Coventry, where anti-aircraft defences were woefully weak. The Germans lost only one bomber that night. (Incidentally, it was claimed long after the war that Coventry was deliberately sacrificed on Churchill's instructions in order to keep secret British knowledge of the enemy's latest blind bombing techniques, and of his target lists, gleaned by way of *Ultra*. There is not a shred of evidence to support this however.)

Meanwhile, the British had devised new airborne radio equipment which enabled aircraft of RAF Bomber Command to fly down the enemy beams and attack the stations which were transmitting them. The first such mission was carried out on the night following the Coventry raid by two Wellingtons of the RAF Wireless Intelligence Unit, one of which achieved a direct hit on the *Knickebein* station at Cherbourg.

By the beginning of 1941, the British scientists had got the measure of X-Apparatus and countermeasures against it were becoming increasingly effective. In fact, by plotting the direction of the enemy radio beams the British were able to pinpoint targets which were scheduled for attack, with inestimable value to the air defences. Once it was realized that the Luftwaffe intended to attack a target in strength, large decoy fires were lit some distance from it, with the result that a high proportion of enemy bombs fell harmlessly in open country.

Early in 1941, the Germans went over to yet another radio beam system known as Y-Apparatus, the operational use of which was again pioneered by the Heinkels of KG100. Whereas X-Apparatus had used three beams crossing on the approach to the target, Y-Apparatus used only one beam in conjunction with a radio signal which told the bomber pilot how far he was along the beam. By this means the pilot was able to keep a continuous check on his progress, dropping his bombs when the correct distance had been flown. Towards the end of 1942 the RAF was to use a similar system known as *Oboe*, although the latter was a good deal more effective than its earlier German counterpart.

In the case of Y-Apparatus, the main obstacle to its success lay in the fact that the British scientists had worked out how it operated even before it became operational, with the result that countermeasures were brought into action from the outset. It was almost certainly due to such countermeasures that enemy bombers attacked Dublin instead of Belfast on the night of 30 May 1941.

From 1942, the main Allied radio countermeasures effort was directed against the German radar-controlled air defence system. The Germans had got off to a slow start in terms of radar defences; although they had experimental GCI (Ground Controlled Interception) stations in place by the end of 1939, and were aware that the British had constructed a chain of radar stations on the south and east coasts, the latter's importance was underestimated by Luftwaffe Intelligence in the Battle of Britain, with the result that they were not attacked as thoroughly as they might have been, luckily for Fighter Command's warning and control system.

The man who gave impetus to German radar development was General Josef Kammhuber, commander of *Fliegerkorps* XII and the Luftwaffe's night-fighter force. Since his appointment in 1940 Kammhuber had striven to weld the German night defences into as efficient an organisation as his resources would permit. He was the architect of a system known as *Himmelbett* (Four-poster bed), a network of overlapping air defence zones extending north–south across the length of occupied Europe, and was a firm advocate of night intruder operations as a means of inflicting the maximum

Chart prepared by RAF Intelligence during the Second World War showing the estimated effective coverage of the German early warning radar chain.

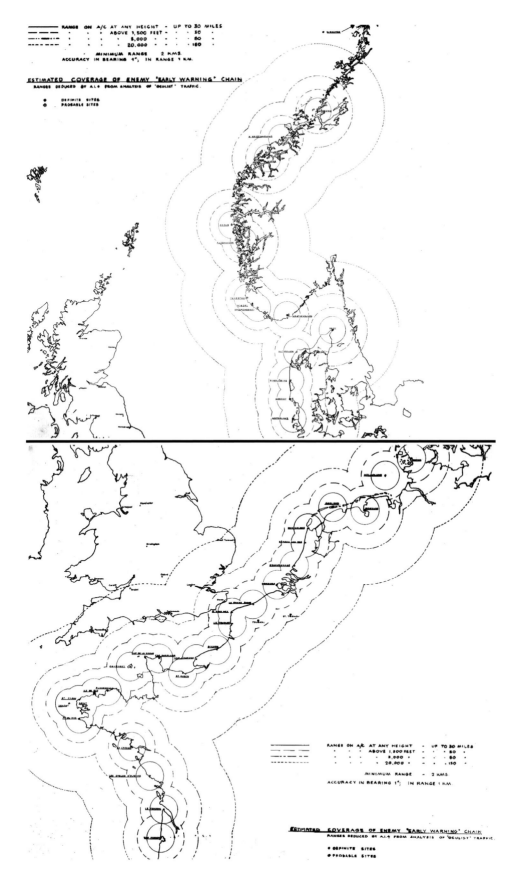

possible damage on the Allied bomber forces. Although what might have become the most potent weapon in his arsenal was knocked from his hand when Hitler personally called a halt to intruder missions over England. Despite the obstacles that confronted him, Kammhuber persevered with his task until by the spring of 1943 he had five *Geschwader* and 400 twin-engined night-fighters under his command on bases from Holland to the Mediterranean.

Thanks to the 'Y' Service, *Ultra* and other sources, the threat presented by the German controlled night-fighter system to the RAF's night bombing offensive was well known by the beginning of 1942, and much had been deduced about its operational methods.

More knowledge was added in February 1942, when one of the system's key components, a *Wurzburg* precision GCI radar, was captured in a commando raid on Bruneval, near Le Havre, and by May 1942 an almost complete and very accurate picture of enemy GCI fighter control had been built up. At the same time, the loss rate suffered on bombing operations was steadily increasing, and there was no doubt that this was due to the large-scale introduction of radar-assisted control of both AA guns and fighters.

The value of radar countermeasures was not in doubt. The development of airborne jamming equipment had been started in late 1941 and was still in progress. One highly effective countermeasure – *Window*, comprising strips of metal foil cut to the wavelength of the German *Freya* area surveillance radar and designed to be dropped in bundles from attacking bombers to confuse the defences – had already been developed, but its use was not yet authorised on the grounds that Britain was still too vulnerable to air attack for the RAF to initiate a jamming war.

By the autumn of 1942, however, losses had become so severe that a continued embargo on radar countermeasures could no longer be justified, and on 6 October a meeting was held at HQ Bomber Command to consider their adoption. The first recommendation was that the bombers' IFF (Identification Friend/Foe) sets be modified to operate on the frequency (120–130 mc/s) of the *Freya* radars so that some jamming could be effected. It was realised that this countermeasure, called *Shiver*, would not achieve much success, so the use of a second radar countermeasure was authorised. This was *Mandrel*, a radar jammer developed at the Wembley laboratories of the General Electric Company. It operated in the 120–130 mc/s band, and two aircraft per squadron were to be fitted with it. Its object was to reduce the range at which the *Freya* sets could identify and plot incoming bombers from 100 to about 25 miles. Two *Mandrel* ground stations, at Dover and Hastings, would also be brought into use to supplement the airborne equipment.

Steps were also taken to disrupt the vital radio communications link between the night-fighters and their ground controllers. This was done by modulating the bombers' transmitters with noise produced by a microphone situated inside the aircraft. Each wireless operator was briefed to search a bank of 150 kc/s between 3 and 6 mc/s and to transmit on the frequency of any German R/T which he heard. This countermeasure, called *Tinsel*, and *Mandrel* were both introduced operationally in December 1942, and a squadron of Boulton Paul Defiants (No. 515) was also equipped with *Mandrel* and given the task of patrolling 50 miles off the enemy coast.

Mandrel was found to be less effective than had been hoped, mainly because the enemy extended the frequency range of the *Freya* from 120–130 mc/s to 120–150 mc/s in an effort to minimise the effect of jamming. They also developed a device called *Freya-Halbe*, which enabled night-fighters to home on to the jamming aircraft, with the result that losses among the *Mandrel*-equipped bombers were high. It was never possible to raise the *Mandrel* barrage to the desired intensity, and although one estimate suggested that a force of 600 *Mandrel*-equipped aircraft would produce the required result, it was never possible, because of a shortage of equipment, to have more than 200 aircraft fitted with the device at any one time.

A greater success was achieved by *Tinsel*, and in April 1943 the 'Y' Service reported that the Germans were making increasing use of VHF radio communications, which operated between 38 and 42 mc/s and was therefore immune to this countermeasure. Another jamming device, *Ground Cigar*, was set up at Sizewell in Suffolk to deal with the new fighter frequency, but it suffered from a lack of range, with a coverage of only 140 miles from the ground station, and it also disrupted the 'Y' Service's VHF traffic. An airborne version was the obvious answer, and development of one – *Airborne Cigar*, more commonly called ABC – was set in motion.

All the frequencies on which the various German ground–air components of the German air defence system operated could be monitored and identified from the United Kingdom, but the short-range airborne interception radars used by the German night-fighters presented a different problem. The first German AI radar, the *Lichtenstein* BC, became operational early in 1942; it operated in the 490 mc/s band and had a maximum range of about two miles.

In July 1942, the 'Y' Service picked up indications that the German night-fighters operating over Holland were using an airborne detection device referred to as *Emil Emil*, but its exact nature could not be ascertained. In an attempt to gather more information, a special duties unit, No. 1474 Flight, was formed, and its Wellingtons, equipped with radio detection gear, began operations over north-west Europe. Seventeen sorties were flown without result; then, on the night of 3/4 December 1942, the radio operator of an 18th Wellington picked up weak signals at 04.30 hr, possibly from German AI radar, on 487 mc/s. The signal strength increased rapidly, and the crew knew that an enemy fighter was locked on to them.

A few moments later the Wellington was heavily attacked by a Junkers 88. The captain of the British aircraft, Pilot Officer Paulton, took evasive action and his rear gunner returned the fire. The specialist radio operator, Pilot Officer Jordan, was badly wounded by the night-fighter's first burst of fire; he nevertheless went on transmitting information about the enemy radar signals back to base for some minutes before he collapsed. The Ju 88 finally broke off the attack when Paulton took the Wellington down in a long dive from 14,000 to 500 feet. The bomber was severely damaged; both its throttles were jammed, its gun turrets were out of action and most of its instruments had been smashed by shell splinters. As the aircraft limped homewards the second specialist wireless operator, Flight Sergeant Bigoray, continued to transmit data, although he was wounded in both legs. The Wellington ditched 200 yards off the British coast and the crew was rescued. For their part in the mission, Plt Off Jordan received the DSO, the pilot was awarded the DFC and Flt Sgt Bigoray the DFM.

The electronic surveillance missions flown by No. 1474 Flight were the first ever of their kind, and led to the development of a jamming device called *Ground Grocer*. This covered only a small area of Holland and Belgium and was of limited value. Of much greater importance was the development by the Telecommunications Research Establishment of *Serrate*, a homing device designed to enable night-fighters to home on to the enemy's *Lichtenstein* transmissions. The range of *Serrate* varied between 50 miles when the *Lichtenstein*'s antenna array was pointing towards it and ten miles

Serrate equipment installed in the nose of a Mosquito.

when it was pointing away. The device was first used operationally by the Bristol Beaufighters of No. 141 Squadron in June 1943, and in the next three months they destroyed 23 enemy aircraft with its help. Normal AI radar was used in the final stages of the interception, and on several occasions German night-fighters came under attack as they themselves were engaged in attacking RAF bombers.

On the night of 24/25 July 1943 Bomber Command used *Window* for the first time in the first of a series of devastating attacks on Hamburg. Its effect was to throw the *Wurzburg* GCI control and gun-laying radars into complete confusion. From then on, *Window* became a primary RCM weapon; no effective antidote to it was ever found. It rendered the *Himmelbett* system of close fighter control virtually impotent and was the final nail in the coffin of General Kammhuber, who had fallen out of favour through his insistence that the night defence of the Reich be given absolute priority. A few weeks later he was replaced as GOC *Fliegerkorps* XII by Major-General Josef Schmidt.

Another direct result of the assault on Hamburg was the release of fighters from the *Himmelbett* zones, allowing them to mix freely with the bomber stream, and the development of the *Wilde Sau* (Wild Boar) concept, in which single-engined day fighters patrolled directly over Germany's cities, their pilots endeavouring to pick out enemy bombers in the glare of searchlights and fires. The idea met with considerable success during the summer and autumn, but the winter months brought unacceptable losses through accidents in bad weather, and the *Wilde Sau* force was disbanded in March 1944.

However, there was no escaping the fact that in the autumn of 1943 Bomber Command's loss rate had once again risen to 80 per cent of the level it had reached prior to the introduction of *Window*, and furthermore British Intelligence was aware

Experimental installation of Monica *radar warning receiver in a Vickers Wellington.*

that the German night-fighter units had begun to equip with the new FUG220 *Lichtenstein* SN-2 AI radar, developed by Telefunken and resistant to both *Window* and the jamming equipment then in use. In the autumn of 1943 two more homing devices were also developed for use by night-fighters, the FUG350 *Naxos Z* and the FUG227 *Flensburg*. The former enabled the fighters to home on transmissions from the RAF's H2S blind bombing radar, and the latter was designed to lock on to radiations from the *Monica* tail warning radar carried by the heavy bombers.

In the early months of 1944 the Allies knew very little about this new equipment, and went to great lengths to gather reliable intelligence data on it. Many perilous sorties were flown by No. 192 Squadron – the former No. 1474 Flight – operating out of Gransden Lodge in Cambridgeshire with a mixture of Wellingtons, Halifaxes and Mosquitos, but with no result. The Mosquitos alone flew 55 sorties in the first three months of the year, five to the Berlin area.

The Germans had unrestricted use of *Lichtenstein* SN-2 for a full six months, during which Bomber Command suffered appalling losses. The only clues to the nature of the new equipment were some signals which had been picked up in the 160 mc/s range and which might have emanated from an AI radar, and a gun-camera photograph, taken by an American fighter, which showed a Ju 88 on the ground featuring a novel type of aerial array. The dimensions of the array, as deduced from the poor-quality photograph, suggested a frequency of around 100 mc/s, which was thought to be too low to produce reliable results. On the assumption – incorrect, as it turned out – that 160 mc/s was likely to be the frequency of the new enemy AI radar, a new type of *Window* called Type Y was produced.

It was never used operationally, for on the night of 12/13 July 1944 a Junkers Ju 88G night-fighter made a serious navigational error and landed at Woodbridge in Suffolk. The aircraft was equipped with both SN-2 AI radar and the *Flensburg* homing device, which were quickly subjected to a thorough evaluation by the Telecommunications Research Establishment. The examination showed that the SN-2 worked on a frequency of around 90 mc/s, and luckily a countermeasure was already available in the form of *Window* Type MB, which had been devised for use in connection with the D-Day landings and which covered all frequencies between 70 and 200 mc/s. Good stocks were still in hand, and on 23/24 July it was dropped on a normal operation. Almost immediately, bomber losses began to decline.

On 8 November 1943 the RAF established a special bomber support force, No. 100 Group, under the command of Air Vice-Marshal E. B. Addison. Its primary functions were to give direct support to Bomber Command by attacking enemy night-fighters, and to employ airborne and ground RCM to jam enemy radio navigational aids, radar systems and wireless signals. With its HQ at West Raynham, No. 100 Group initially comprised three squadrons (Nos 141, 169 and 239) transferred from Fighter Command. These were joined in March 1944 by No. 515 Squadron. By the summer of 1944 these four squadrons were armed with Mosquito night-fighters, all equipped with *Serrate* for bomber support operations except No. 515, which operated in the night intruder role.

By the time No. 100 Group was formed, several countermeasures were deployed operationally with Bomber Command. In addition to *Window, Mandrel* and *Ground Cigar*, there was *Airborne Cigar*, first used operationally in the Lancasters of No. 101 Squadron on the night of 7/8 October 1943. Each was fitted with a panoramic receiver and three transmitters, and carried a specially-trained German-speaking ABC operator in addition to the normal crew. The operator listened for German fighter control communications, and jammed any transmissions that were picked up. To add to the jamming potential in the 3–6 mc/s band, a countermeasure known as *Corona* was also set up. Four *Corona* ground stations were established, using high-powered GPO transmitters to issue false instructions to the German night-fighter force. The BBC transmitter at Crowborough, the most powerful in Europe, was also used for jamming under the code-name *Dartboard*. Another countermeasure, *Ground Grocer*, began operations at Dunwich in Suffolk in April 1944, its function being to jam enemy AI signals on 490–500 mc/s.

Several problems were experienced in the creation of No. 100 Group's RCM force. The first lay in the choice of a suitable aircraft, which had to be big enough to carry the necessary equipment and be able to fly fast and high enough to stand a chance of avoiding night-fighters. The aircraft selected eventually was the Boeing B-17 Flying Fortress, which was considered to meet all the requirements. Fourteen B-17Fs were obtained, and necessary modifications were carried out early in 1944 by the Scottish Aviation Company at Prestwick. These included the replacement of the Fortress's chin turret by an H2S blister, the provision of mufflers to screen the exhaust flames and the fitting of the jamming devices in the bomb bay. The aircraft began operations with No. 214 Squadron in June 1944. In addition, B-17s of the 803rd Squadron, United States Strategic Air Forces, were also equipped for the jamming role, and this unit was placed under the operational control of No. 100 Group.

The RCM equipment carried by these aircraft was called *Jostle* and *Piperack*. The first, a high-powered communications jammer, emitted a high-pitched wail and could effectively jam any frequency used by the German fighter controllers; the second,

Jostle *ECM jamming equipment installed in a Short Stirling.*

developed from an American RCM kit called *Dina*, designed to reinforce *Mandrel*, covered the 90–110 mc/s frequency used by the German AI radars. A third squadron, No. 223, which was equipped with Liberators and which began operations in September 1944, was also equipped with these devices. *Mandrel* operations, which did not require fast, high-flying aircraft since they were usually conducted clear of enemy territory, were flown by the Stirlings of No. 199 Squadron and the Halifaxes of No. 171, joined at the end of 1944 by the Halifaxes of No. 642 Squadron. No. 192 Squadron, meanwhile, continued to monitor enemy radio and radar transmissions, and in late 1944 it wasted a lot of effort in searching for the radio signals that were mistakenly thought to guide V-2 rockets.

In their finalised form, the tactics used by No. 100 Group's RCM force were as follows. *Mandrel*-equipped aircraft, employed mainly to provide a screen for the main bomber force, would operate in pairs with 14 miles between them, forming a line positioned some 80 miles from enemy territory. With their *Mandrels* switched on, the orbiting aircraft formed an effective electronic curtain through which the enemy search radars were unable to penetrate. Aircraft equipped with *Jostle* and *Piperack*, on the other hand, flew 4,000 feet above the bomber stream at intervals of ten miles, providing an electronic umbrella to disrupt the German AI radar and voice communications.

The Germans tried desperately to remain a step ahead of Allied countermeasures developments. Early in 1944 they began work on two new types of AI radar, the FUG 218 *Neptun* VR and the FUG 228 *Lichtenstein* SN-3. The former worked in the 163–187 mc/s band, the latter in the 100–112 mc/s band, and the frequencies of both could be altered in

Jostle *ECM aerial installation in a B-25 Mitchell.*

the air to make jamming more difficult. Production of the SN-3 had already started when the Allies found an effective means of jamming the German *Freya* ground radar, which worked on the same waveband, so further work on the SN-3 AI set was stopped and production concentrated on *Neptun*. This was first used operationally in February 1945, but the Allies quickly discovered that it was vulnerable to *Window* of the right length and within three weeks effective countermeasures had been devised against it.

By the end of the war the Allies had built up a highly effective and experienced RCM force, and there can be no doubt that it played a key role in their air victory over North West Europe. The equipment developed under the pressures of combat, and the operational techniques devised for its use, formed the bases of every future development in the field of electronic warfare.

It is therefore extraordinary, that for a full five years after the end of the Second World War, the vital role of electronic air surveillance was pushed into a back seat to the extent that it almost slid out of sight. The result was an intelligence vacuum that took many years – and cost many lives – to fill. It might have cost the western world its freedom.

Opposite, top: Rebecca *aerial installation under the nose of a Wellington. A homing device,* Rebecca *was originally developed for use by special duties squadrons to pick up transmissions from reka ground beacons on supply dropping operations in occupied countries.*

Opposite, bottom: *What appears to be an early fire control system under test in a Fortress II at RAF Defford, sometime in 1944.*

3

US Strategic Air Intelligence, 1945–50

WHEN THE UNITED States entered the war in December 1941, following the Japanese attack on Pearl Harbor, it soon became apparent that both the US Navy and the Army Air Forces were seriously deficient in photographic reconnaissance facilities. In the case of the Navy, long-range aircraft such as the Catalina were used for visual reconnaissance and were not equipped with cameras until much later. The situation improved after the summer of 1942, when the Army agreed to provide the Navy with a number of B-24 Liberators, some of which were fitted with cameras under the designation F-7 and F-7A. These aircraft saw widespread operational use in the South Pacific, photo-mapping Japanese-held islands prior to an Allied assault. Infrared and colour photography, still comparatively rare, were used to pick out camouflaged targets. On 4 February 1944, two Liberators of VMD-254 made a twelve-hour night flight from the Solomon Islands to photograph Truk in preparation for a carrier strike later in the month, and on 18 April PR Liberators of VD-3 made a 13-hour round flight to photograph Saipan, Tinian and Aguijan Islands in preparation for the campaign to occupy the Marianas. They were accompanied by Army Air Force B-24s, which bombed the islands as a diversion.

Because of the rudimentary nature of the Japanese air defence system, there was never a priority requirement in the Pacific theatre for electronic intelligence gathering and the development of associated countermeasures systems. However, under a project called *Cadillac II*, sponsored by the US Government and undertaken by the Massachusetts Institute of Technology (MIT), 32 B-17G Flying Fortresses were fitted out as airborne Combat Information Centres (CIC) as a countermeasure against *Kamikaze* suicide attacks. Designated PB-1W in US Navy service, these aircraft carried an AN/APS 20B search radar in a large belly radome and had a limited fighter direction capability over a range of about 65 miles against low-flying aircraft, and 200 miles against shipping.

The Army Air Forces in the Pacific initially used the B-24 Liberator in the long range strategic reconnaissance role under the designation F-7. F-7A conversions totalled 182 aircraft, these carrying eleven cameras mounted in the nose, bomb bay and rear fuselage. The F-7B, 32 of which were converted from B-24Js, carried six bomb bay cameras. Reconnaissance of the Japanese home islands in the closing months of the war was carried out by the PR variant of the Boeing B-29 Superfortress, the F-13.

The first USAAF PR unit to deploy to the European theatre was the 3rd Photo Group under Colonel Elliott Roosevelt, which arrived at Steeple Morden in Cambridgeshire

The Lockheed F-5G PR version of the P-38 Lightning carried five cameras in a special nose section that could be interchanged with the regular production nose section that carried the fighter's armament.

in September 1942 and departed for North Africa two months later. The Group at first used B-17s (F-9s) and Lockheed P-38Es (F-4s), but soon converted to P-38G/Hs, known as F-5As. By the end of 1944 three reconnaissance groups were operational in the Mediterranean theatre, while the Eighth and Ninth Air Forces in England had 20 reconnaissance squadrons at their disposal, equipped with F-5s, F-6s (the PR version of the P-51 Mustang) and de Havilland Mosquito Mk XVIs, the latter serving with the 25th Bombardment Group at Watton in Norfolk.

The 25th BG was formed from the 803rd Squadron, whose countermeasures role under the control of No. 100 Group RAF has already been mentioned. The USAAF's first electronic intelligence mission, however, was not flown over North West Europe. On 6 March 1943, a modified B-24D Liberator code-named *Ferret 1* made an electronic intelligence flight over the Aleutian Islands to gather information on Japanese radar in Kiska. The name 'Ferret' stuck, and was applied to all subsequent missions of this nature. In the Mediterranean theatre, B-24s of the 16th Reconnaissance Squadron flew many sorties in preparation for, and in support of, the Allied landings on Sicily and in southern Italy pinpointing no fewer than 450 enemy radar sites.

The 16th RS also pioneered the use of the RC-156 jammer, which was designed at Harvard's Radio Research Laboratory and which was known as *Carpet*. Meant to close any gaps that might appear when *Window* was being used, *Carpet* was designed to jam the *Wurzburg* gun-laying radars, and operated in their frequency band of 530–580 mc/s.

Designed in 1943 to meet a precise requirement for a long-range photo-reconnaissance aircraft, the Republic XR-12 Rainbow had an excellent high-altitude performance. Two prototypes were built.

As soon as the receiver picked up a *Wurzburg* signal the jamming was applied on that frequency for two minutes, after which the receiver continued to search. Any signals received were presumed to be from a *Wurzburg* tracking the RCM aircraft, so *Carpet* was especially designed for the protection of the carrier. The device was used extensively by the USAAF with a great deal of success and was also used by the RAF from March 1944, but by that time the Germans were taking steps to counter *Carpet* jamming by widening the *Wurzburg* frequency band and Bomber Command never derived much benefit from it.

At the end of the Second World War, three types of dedicated photo-reconnaissance aircraft were under development in the United States. The first was the Northrop F-15A Reporter, which was developed from the P-61 Black Widow night-fighter and which, like its predecessor, was a twin-engined, twin-boom design. The F-15A, which had an excellent performance at high altitude, was ordered by the USAAF and first flew in June 1945, but only 36 had been built at the war's end and the original contract for 175 aircraft was cancelled. It never saw operational service.

The second type was the Republic XR-12 (previously designated XF-12) Rainbow, one of the most beautifully streamlined aircraft ever built. Designed in 1943 to a very precise requirement drawn up by the USAAF's Photographic Section of the Air Technical Service, it was powered by four massive 3,500 hp Pratt & Whitney R-4360 Wasp Major radial engines to give it a top speed of 400 mph or more at over 40,000 feet. The first of two prototypes flew on 4 February 1946 and was extensively tested, but as the war was over the programme was no longer considered urgent and the second aircraft did not fly until August 1947. This example carried a full photographic fit in three camera compartments and was equipped with a laboratory so that photographs could be processed in flight. It was destroyed on 4 November 1948 when its number two engine exploded during a test flight. By this time the USAF (as the USAAF had now become) requirement had been withdrawn, and the only reason testing of the two Rainbows had continued for so long was to assess the aircraft's suitability as a long-range transatlantic airliner, Pan American Airways having shown an interest.

The third aircraft, designed to the same specification as the Rainbow, was the Hughes XR-11 (formerly XF-11), which like the F-15A was a twin-engined, twin-boom monoplane. It was developed from an earlier Howard Hughes design, the unsuccessful D-2 high speed, long-range bomber that was constructed from Duramold, a plastic impregnated wood product. The XR-11 was a large aircraft, with a wingspan of 101 feet, and its airframe was completely streamlined, with every rivet flush and every join smoothed and sanded. It was sprayed with a shiny nylon-based clear coat which, when dried, was heavily waxed and polished to add a few more knots to the maximum speed.

The prototype XR-11 flew on 7 July 1946, with Hughes himself at the controls, but it suffered a propeller failure on an early test flight and crashed into Beverly Hills. Hughes was seriously injured, but recovered to fly the second prototype on 5 April 1947.

Like the other projects, the XR-11 died in its infancy, the victim of post-war economy, altered requirements and progress, for this was now the age of the jet aircraft, and piston-engined reconnaissance aircraft, even at 40,000 feet and 450 mph, were no longer immune to interception. Yet in the early years of what was to become known as the Cold War, these were the only aircraft available to the Western alliance as it strove to assemble intelligence on the capability of a new and formidable potential enemy, the Soviet Union.

As relations between east and west worsened, one area of particular concern to the Americans and British was the development of Soviet strategic bombers. As the Second World War drew to a close the Chief Administration of the Soviet Air Force, already mindful of changing political forces that would almost certainly lead to an East–West confrontation of some sort in the early post-war years, had plans in hand for the updating of all combat elements, and these included the formation of a modern strategic bombing force. With the wartime emphasis very much on the development of tactical bombers, assault aircraft and fighters, Soviet designers had had little time to study long-range bomber projects, and it was obvious that even if work on such projects began in 1944 there would still be a dangerous gap before a Soviet strategic bomber could be produced in series. Then, suddenly, a ready-made answer literally fell out of the sky in the shape of a Boeing B-29 Superfortress of the USAAF's 58th Bomb Group, which made an emergency landing on Russian territory after an attack on a Japanese target in Manchuria. Before the end of 1944, the Russians had acquired three more B-29s in similar fashion.

By copying the B-29 in every detail, the Russians hoped to avoid all the technological problems associated with the development of an aircraft of this kind. The designer chosen for the task was Andrei N. Tupolev, while the job of copying the B-29's Wright R-3350 engines went to A. M. Shvetsov. The work was not easy; major snags cropped up frequently, particularly in connection with electronically-controlled equipment such as the B-29's gun turrets. Despite everything, however, construction of the Russian B-29 copy – designated Tu-4 – was begun in March 1945, and the first of three prototypes would be ready for flight testing within two years.

Reports that reached US Intelligence of Russian developments in the strategic bomber field were at best vague, and although there was enough evidence to show that work was in progress the Americans would not become aware that a copy of the B-29 was involved until 1948, when the three Tu-4 prototypes were publicly revealed at the big Soviet air display at Tushino, near Moscow. What was clear in 1946, though, was that if the Russians were developing a bomber capable of launching an attack against the continental United States, such an attack would have to be made from bases in the Soviet Arctic, the aircraft relying on navigational aids positioned at forward sites in the polar regions, or from the Kamchatka Peninsula in the Far East.

Thanks to a series of well-publicised survey flights made in the 1930s, ostensibly to gather information for setting up a direct long-range air route to the United States, the Russians knew more about the Arctic than anyone else. The Americans, on the other hand, knew comparatively little, and this gap in their knowledge they were now anxious to fill. In March 1946, therefore, the 46th Reconnaissance Squadron (Very Long Range) was deployed to Ladd Air Force Base in Alaska. Equipped with ten B-29s (including a couple of F-13s fitted out for photo-reconnaissance), the 46th RS came under the operational control of the 311th Reconnaissance Wing, which in turn was assigned to the USAF Strategic Air Command, established on 21 March 1946. Following a series of preliminary survey flights over the Arctic by the 46th RS, which mainly involved the checking and upgrading of navigational equipment, the 28th Bomb Group, a B-29 unit stationed at Grand Island Army Air Field, Nebraska, deployed to Elmendorf in Alaska for a six-month period of training in arctic conditions.

Meanwhile, a detachment of the 311th RW, known as the East Reconnaissance Group, SAC, equipped with F-9 (B-17) photo-mapping aircraft and based at Thule, had begun the aerial mapping of Greenland. This mission was expanded in the following year into Operation *Eardrum*, with aircraft of the 311th RW surveying the polar area between Iceland and Alaska. In July 1947 the 311th RW received its first two F-13As (RB-29s), which were fully equipped for photographic and electronic reconnaissance; these aircraft (serials 44-61583 and 44-61999) were delivered to the 7th Geodectic Control Squadron of the 311th RW at MacDill Army Air Field, Florida, but a month later they were transferred to the 16th Photo Squadron (Special) to begin intelligence-gathering flights.

In October 1947 the 46th RS was redesignated the 72nd Strategic Reconnaissance Squadron; this was part of a substantial reorganisation that took place following the creation of the United States Air Force in September. Within a year aircraft designations were also altered, the F-13A officially becoming the RB-29 in June 1948.

In 1948–9 the 72nd SRS carried out many photographic reconnaissance and ELINT missions over the Soviet Arctic and the Far East, its RB-29s equipped with oblique cameras that enabled them to photograph Russian territory while remaining in international air space. These long-range photographs, however, revealed little that was of use, and by the end of 1948 some RB-29s, stripped of all weapons and other unnecessary equipment to give them extra altitude, were making penetration flights into the Soviet Union on behalf of the US Central Intelligence Agency, such flights being authorised by the US president, Harry S. Truman. The first overflight was carried out on 5 August, 1948, when a 72nd SRS RB-29 took off from Ladd AFB, made a surveillance flight over Siberia, and landed at Yokota AB, Japan, after a total time in the air of 19 hours and 40 minutes.

Flights of similar duration – and even on occasions of up to 30 hours – quickly became routine, the aircraft operating at 35,000 feet or more on missions that sometimes covered 5,000 miles. Before long, gaps in the Soviet radar coverage – which at this stage was quite rudimentary – were established, and RB-29 crews exploited such corridors to the full as they penetrated Russian territory. Sometimes, however, the RB-29s were detected and fighters sent up to intercept them, but until the MiG-15 entered service late in 1948 (and then only with trials units based in the western USSR) the Russians had no fighter that could touch them.

While the RB-29s carried out their photographic and electronic surveillance of the Soviet Union, officials of the US Atomic Energy Commission were expressing fears that the United States had little or no intelligence on the Soviet Union's nuclear research programme. The Russians had been actively researching nuclear physics since the 1930s, and in February 1939, when Russian scientists learned of the discovery of nuclear fission from scientific papers published in foreign journals, the military significance was immediately recognised. By April 1939 Soviet scientists had independently established that each split uranium nucleus emitted between two and four neutrons, and that a chain reaction was therefore possible. By 1940 they had concluded that a chain reaction could be established using either uranium-235 or natural uranium, and a moderator such as heavy water (deuterium oxide).

In June 1940 the Uranium Commission was established by the Praesidium of the Soviet Academy of Sciences to conduct research into the 'uranium problem'. Work was to proceed on a broad front that included exploring for uranium deposits, production of heavy water, construction of a cyclotron and so on. This research proceeded at a slow pace during the next year, and was halted completely following the German invasion, but early in 1942 the Soviet leadership began to pay serious attention to the possibility of producing an atomic bomb as a result of intelligence information about British, American and German work in the field. Although concerned about development costs, Stalin nevertheless initiated a small-scale project in 1943 under the direction of a noted scientist, Igor Vasilievich Kurchatov.

Kurchatov drew up a research plan with three main objectives: to achieve a chain reaction in an experimental reactor using natural uranium; to develop methods of isotope separation; and to study the design of both the U-235 and plutonium bombs. By the end of 1943 50 scientists were working in his laboratory, a figure that doubled in the course of the following year. By the time of the Potsdam Conference between the wartime Allied leaders, which coincided with the testing of the first US nuclear device on 16 July 1945, the Soviet Union had a serious atomic bomb project well under way. On 24 July, eight days after the US test, President Truman told Stalin after one conference session that the United States had a 'new weapon of unusual destructive force'. Stalin told Truman he hoped the United States 'would make good use of it against the Japanese'. He also instructed Kurchatov to speed up his research work.

Following the atomic attacks on Hiroshima and Nagasaki in August 1945, according to the Soviet Military supremo Marshal Zhukov, Stalin ordered Kurchatov to 'provide us with atomic weapons in the shortest possible time', and placed his chief of secret police, Lavrenti Beria, in charge of the project.

American concern about the development of Soviet atomic weapons led to the creation, in 1947, of a Long Range Detection Program and the establishment by the USAF of an airborne monitoring system capable of detecting and pinpointing a nuclear detonation within the main Soviet land mass or the Arctic. A number of WB-29 weather reconnaissance aircraft were equipped with air sampling boxes containing filters about the size of an eight by ten-inch photographic plate, designed to collect radioactive particles from the atmosphere. The plates were changed every hour, and the aircraft's track during each period was recorded.

On 3 September 1949, long hours of patrol work at last paid dividends. A WB-29 flying at 18,000 feet between Japan and Alaska detected an unusual amount of radioactive debris, and the finding was confirmed by other WB-29 flights elsewhere in the world. Analysis of the particles by US atomic physicists revealed traces of the same kind of radioactive debris produced by American nuclear tests. It was clear that somewhere in the Asiatic land mass, the Russians had tested a nuclear device.

The news of the Russian test, which the Americans named *Joe 1*, was announced by President Truman on 23 September. Until about the middle of 1953, the Americans believed it had taken place on 27 August 1949; the actual date was 29 August. The apparent location of the test was in the general vicinity of the Aral Sea, although another estimate put it roughly on the northeast shore of the Caspian Sea. The time of the test was reported as 17.00 hr local; plutonium was used as the fissionable material, and the US scientists deduced that it was a tower shot, indicating that it was a device rather than a finished bomb. In fact, the test had taken place a long way from the Aral and Caspian Seas, at the Semipalatinsk test site in Eastern Kazakhstan, an area bounded by coordinates 49 52N to 50 08N, and 77 42E to 79 06E. It was here that most of the Soviet Union's uranium deposits were concentrated.

In the year before the first Russian atomic test, East–West relations had taken a severe turn for the worse following the Soviet blockade of Berlin, which began in June 1948 and ended in the summer of 1949. With a real risk of the situation escalating into all-out war, the United States military commitment in Europe was greatly increased, and surveillance flights along the USSR's western frontiers stepped up. Many ELINT missions during this period were flown by the US Navy's PB4Y-2 Privateer maritime patrol aircraft, usually deployed to Port Lyautey in French Morocco. From there, single aircraft detachments were sent to Germany for surveillance flights over the Baltic, while other Privateers monitored the Black Sea and the Adriatic.

On 8 April 1950, a Privateer of Patrol Squadron VP-26 (Captain Lt Jack Fette) took off from Wiesbaden and headed out over the Baltic, its mission to gather intelligence on Soviet naval installations and communications on the coast of Latvia. Somewhere off the port of Libau, it was intercepted by Russian fighters – variously claimed to be La-9s, La-11s or MiG-15s – and shot down with the loss of all ten crew. The Russians stated that the aircraft (which they said was a B-29) had been destroyed after it had penetrated Soviet air space and ignored instructions to land, which was patently untrue; if it had been shot down over land it would have been identified as a Privateer, which bore no resemblance to the B-29 other than it also had four engines. In fact, the aircraft had been a good ten miles off the coast when it was shot down – a little too close for comfort, perhaps, but still over international waters.

ELINT aircraft had been intercepted before, and on one occasion fired at; that was on 22 October 1949, when an La-9 – one of a pair which intercepted an RB-29 over the Sea of Japan – fired a warning burst across the Superfortresses's bows. The Privateer incident was different. It was a clear warning from the Russians that in future, any ELINT aircraft that came too close to its sensitive areas might expect no mercy.

A month after the loss of the Privateer, the US Joint Chiefs of Staff issued an instruction ordering surveillance aircraft to remain at least 20 miles clear of hostile territory, and the US President himself forbade any penetrations of Soviet air space.

The ink on these orders was barely dry when, in the Far East, America's strategic air intelligence services faced their sternest test so far.

4

Air Intelligence in the Korean War

IT WAS DURING the Korean War, which erupted when communist North Korean forces crossed the 38th Parallel to invade the Republic of Korea on 25 June 1950, that serious deficiencies in the USAF's reconnaissance system, both strategic and tactical, became apparent. Rapid intervention by American forces prevented the North Korean Army from securing a swift victory, and by October 1950 the NKA, battered mercilessly by air power, had been pushed back across the parallel; but Chinese combat units now joined the battle, and the Allied counter-offensive was brought to a halt.

American Intelligence sources gravely underestimated the number of Chinese troops in Korea at the end of October 1950. US Eighth Army G-2, Far East Command Intelligence and the Central Intelligence Agency all agreed that the number of Chinese Communist Forces (CCF) in Korea at that time did not exceed 60,000, but in fact more than 180,000 Chinese troops had already entered North Korea from Manchuria. It was only when Allied troops in the front line began to suffer heavy and repeated setbacks at the hands of vastly superior communist forces that the serious nature of the error was appreciated.

There were two reasons for this lack of Intelligence. The first was that the CCF were adept at moving across country in small groups at night to reach their assembly areas, and in the almost complete absence of an Allied spy network in North Korea these movements went undetected. The second was the critical shortage of air reconnaissance assets, a problem compounded by the fact that the Allies had no detailed and accurate maps of the north – a serious shortcoming when it came to interpreting aerial photographs and relating their content to the surrounding terrain.

On the outbreak of hostilities in Korea, HQ Far East Air Forces did not possess any effective air reconnaissance system. Its sole reconnaissance capability, discounting two RB-17s of the 6204th Photo-Mapping Flight at Clark Air Base, in the Philippines, lay with six Boeing RB-29s of the 31st Strategic Reconnaissance Squadron, Very Long Range (VLR) – a US Strategic Air Command unit – at Kadena, on the island of Okinawa, and the RF-80A Shooting Stars of the 8th Tactical Reconnaissance Squadron at Yokota, Japan, but no real plans existed for their operational use in the event of war, and their effectiveness suffered as a consequence. This meant that FEAF had to build up a reconnaissance system from scratch, which was a slow process. A third reconnaissance unit, the 167th TRS (Night Photography) with Douglas RB-26s, arrived at Itazuke, Japan, towards the end of August 1950, but the next unit to arrive, the 45th TRS operating North American RF-51 Mustangs, was not able to begin operations from Itazuke until November because of a shortage of aircraft. The 45th TRS's role

Boeing B-29 bombers being serviced and armed for a mission to North Korea, 1950.

was visual battlefield reconnaissance, and until it began operations this task was carried out on behalf of the Eighth Army almost entirely by North American T-6 Texans, their crews running incredible risks to secure information.

For some months after the beginning of hostilities the 31st SRS's RB-29s operated with impunity over North Korea, and with the first rumours of Chinese intervention they concentrated on the north-western sector, from where their crews could monitor the clutch of Chinese airfields just across the Yalu river in Manchuria. Monitoring was all they could do, for United Nations aircraft were strictly forbidden to cross the river to press home attacks on airfield targets. On 18 October 1950 one RB-29 crew reported that 75 fighters were parked in neat rows on Antung airfield. The next morning they had gone, but their brief presence was an indication that the Chinese might be about to become involved in the Korean air war.

It was not a bluff. On 1 November, six Russian-built MiG-15 jet fighters crossed the Yalu and engaged a flight of Mustangs, and on the 9th two MiGs attacked a flak-damaged RB-29 over Sinuiju. One of the enemy jets was shot down by Corporal Harry J. LeVene, the RB-29's tail gunner, but the other MiG inflicted more damage on the American aircraft, which limped back to Johnson Air Base in Japan, where five crew members were killed in a crash landing. After this experience FEAF forbade its RB-29s to operate in the vicinity of the Yalu, the reconnaissance task in this area being taken on by the RF-80As. These aircraft, incidentally, were also involved in making short-penetration runs over Soviet territory, notably Sakhalin Island.

On 16 November 1950 the 31st SRS was redesignated the 91st SRS, which continued to operate RB-29s from Okinawa. Since July 1950 the 91st SRS, based at Barksdale AFB in Louisiana, had been re-equipping with the Boeing RB-50, a much improved variant of the RB-29, but in this paper transaction the more modern aircraft remained in the USA.

In December 1950, because of the urgent need to acquire photographic intelligence,

The North American B-45 Tornado, seen in company with the Korean War's famous fighter, the F-86 Sabre. The RB-45C version of the Tornado had a 'solid' nose.

FEAF once again authorised the 91st SRS's RB-29s to undertake missions over northwestern Korea with a promise of fighter escort by F-80s, but this plan had to be altered when the Chinese winter offensive compelled the Allied fighter wings to withdraw to Japan, leaving only detachments behind to service and rearm aircraft on combat missions over Korea. On 31 January 1951, in an attempt to fill the strategic reconnaissance gap, FEAF Bomber Command assumed control of Reconnaissance Detachment A, 84th Bombardment Squadron, which had been operating a pair of North American RB-45C aircraft on trials over Korea for the past three months. The four-jet RB-45C, which had a radar mapping facility as well as cameras, could operate at 38,000 feet at 0.72M, so it had a far better chance of survival than the RB-29. The RB-45Cs operated over the Yalu from the beginning of the Chinese intervention in Korea, and one of the original pair was shot down on 12 December 1950 with the loss of its crew. With Bomber Command, the RB-45Cs were assigned to the 91st SRS and continued to provide valuable intelligence throughout the war. A superb aircraft to fly, the RB-45C was manoeuvrable at altitude and was usually able to outrun pursuing fighters, although there were some narrow escapes; on 9 April 1951, for example, an RB-45C was intercepted by four MiG-15s which continued to attack it until they had used up all their ammunition, amazingly without obtaining any hits.

In the summer of 1951, with the battlefront in Korea becoming stabilised and fighter squadrons re-occupying Korean airfields, RB-29 missions over northwestern Korea were resumed under strong fighter escort, but losses continued to mount and in October these operations were again halted. Daylight missions by RB-45Cs with fighter escort were allowed to continue, but on 9 November 1951 an unescorted RB-45C was attacked by nine MiG-15s near Haeju, and escaped only because of exceptionally poor communist gunnery. After this, the RB-45Cs were no longer permitted to make daylight penetrations into 'MiG Alley', as northwestern Korea was known.

In the winter of 1951–52, because of heavy losses inflicted on FEAF Bomber Command's B-29 force by the MiG-15s and flak during daylight operations, the emphasis switched to night bombing, and this revealed a serious deficiency in bombing techniques and equipment. The 91st SRS's RB-45Cs, although equipped for radar mapping, could not be used for night photography because they buffeted too badly when the forward bomb bay was opened to drop flash bombs. The problem was that Bomber Command needed bomb damage assessment photography as quickly as possible after an attack, so that if necessary the target could be attacked again before the enemy had time to strengthen his defences, and this required night reconnaissance. In January 1952, the RB-45Cs were therefore assigned to daylight operations over northeastern Korea, where MiG-15s were seldom encountered, and the 91st SRS was directed to convert its RB-29s to night photography.

It was when the aircraft were sent out on operations that the problems began to mount. For safety reasons, and also to enable them to receive accurate directions from ground-based Shoran (short range navigation radar), they had to fly at altitudes of over 20,000 feet. From such heights the standard M-46 photoflash bomb did not provide adequate illumination, and the camera equipment could not secure photographs of sufficiently large scale for accurate interpretation. The situation improved somewhat with the arrival of more powerful M-120 photoflash bombs in July 1952, but no new camera equipment was forthcoming and results remained undependable.

In addition to air reconnaissance, the 91st SRS also carried out a vital electronic countermeasures role, the development of which was accelerated after June 1952, as enemy air defences became stronger and more proficient and new search and GCI radars, hitherto unsuspected, were identified. In this it was assisted by detachments of the 343rd Strategic Reconnaissance Squadron from Alaska and the 324th SRS from Yokota, Japan, whose RB-29s were better equipped with electronic intelligence receivers. Data on enemy radars and electronic systems, collected by the 'ferret' RB-29s, was collated, evaluated and disseminated by a special section of the 548th Reconnaissance Technical Squadron. Despite the use of old equipment and partly-trained operators, FEAF Bomber Command's ECM programme produced results. Between 1 January and 27 July 1953, in the course of 534 B-29 sorties, 114 aircraft were illuminated by searchlights, and in at least 87 cases the searchlight radar lock was broken by the use of ECM. Had ECM not been available, Bomber Command's losses would almost certainly have been triple what they were.

As it was, they were bad enough. Between 18 November 1952 and 31 January 1953 the communist air defences achieved notable successes at night, destroying five B-29s and damaging three more so badly that they had to be withdrawn from service. In the words of the official USAF history of the USAF in Korea:

'On the night of 18/19 November 1952 the Reds revealed new tactics when they shot down a 98th Wing B-29 coming off its supply-centre target at Sonchon. Riding above the B-29, a Red spotter dropped flares every time the bomber changed direction. The flares allowed searchlights to lock on the bomber, and four Red fighter passes riddled the bomber, forcing its crew to abandon ship over Cho-do. On the night of 30/31 December, when a full moon was at its zenith and contrails were streaming at bombing altitudes, Red searchlights coned three 19th Group B-29s which were attacking an ore-processing plant near the Yalu at Choak-tong. A conventional airplane called signals from above the bombers, and Red fighters shot down one B-29 and damaged two others so badly that their crews were forced down at Suwon. Bomber Command blamed the moonlight and the contrails for the losses, but in the dark of the moon on the night of 10/11 January 1953 a 307th Wing B-29 was coned by searchlights, hit by flak, and shot down by fighters over Anju's marshalling yards. The position of this bomber was apparently betrayed by light contrails.

On the night of 12 January Red fighters intercepted and shot down a lone 91st Reconnaissance Squadron RB-29 which was distributing leaflets along the Yalu. On 28/29 January enemy fighters apparently silhouetted a 19th Group B-29 against a full moon over Kimpodong and needed no other illumination to shoot it down. Moonlight again betrayed 307th Wing B-29s when they bombed the Unjong-ni supply area on the night of 30/31 January. Some ten Red fighters prosecuted attacks which so badly damaged a B-29 that it barely managed an emergency landing in South Korea. The total number of Red interceptions was not great. Bomber Command reported only 20 non-firing and 23 firing passes made against its aircraft in January 1953. But the Red night interceptions were becoming extremely effective. Darkness was no longer affording the old B-29s the protection they needed to attack targets in North Korea...'

Nevertheless, FEAF Bomber Command was to lose no more B-29s to enemy action after January 1953. This was partly due to natural causes, such as the raising of the contrail-forming level with the onset of spring, but other countermeasures were brought into play, including bomber support by intruder night-fighters: the Douglas F3D-2N Skynights of Marine Fighter Squadron VMF(N)-513 and the Lockheed F-94 Starfires of the USAF's 319th Fighter Interceptor Squadron.

In addition to ECM operations over Korea, and occasional penetrations of Chinese airspace, the 91st SRS also undertook numerous long-range 'ferret' missions off the north-east coastline of the Soviet Union, the RB-29s flying from Japan on a route that took them via Vladivostok, Sakhalin, the Sea of Okhotsk and Kamchatka before crossing the Bering Sea to land and refuel in Alaska, where detachments of the 38th and 343rd SRS (both components of the 55th Strategic Reconnaissance Wing) were located, before making the return trip. Such operations were hazardous; on 13 June 1952 an RB-29 vanished without trace over the Sea of Japan, the presumed victim of Russian fighters, and on 7 October another RB-29 was attacked and destroyed by MiG-15s while flying at 15,000 feet in the same area. On 15 March 1953, a third RB-29, this one belonging to the 38th SRS and flown by Lt Col Robert Rich, was attacked by a MiG while it was operating 100 miles northeast of the Soviet naval base of Petropavlovsk on Kamchatka, but on this occasion the reconnaissance aircraft escaped after the Russian fighter was beaten off by the tail gunner, T/Sgt Jesse Prim, and landed safely in Alaska.

Douglas F3D Skynights of Marine Fighter Squadron VMF(N)-513 were used in the bomber support role over Korea.

The Lockheed F-94C Starfire also took the war to the enemy in the night skies of Korea.

The United States Navy's long-range reconnaissance commitment in the Far East during the Korean War was fulfilled mainly by by the Martin PBM-5 Mariners of Patrol Squadron VP-47, the Lockheed P2V Neptunes of VP-6 and VP-22, and the Convair PB4Y-2 Privateers of VP-772 and VP-871; Short Sunderlands of the RAF's Far East Flying Boat Wing also patrolled the west coast of Korea. The Mariners, covering eight patrol areas on missions lasting up to twelve hours, located and tracked hundreds of ships. Enemy fighters were occasionally encountered; on 31 July 1951 a Mariner was attacked by two MiG-15s, whose fire killed two crew members and wounded two others, and on 26 May 1953 another PBM patrolling Wonsan Harbour was approached from astern by an unidentified aircraft, which was driven off by the Mariner's tail gunner.

It was the Neptunes, however, that flew most of the 'ferret' operations on behalf of the US Navy, and they paid an inevitable price. On 6 November 1951 a P2V of VP-6, carrying out what was officially described as a 'weather reconnaissance mission over international waters off Siberia' was attacked and shot down by MiG-15s, and on 18 January 1953 a Neptune of VP-22 was shot down off Swatow Island in the Formosa Straits by Red Chinese AA fire. Rescue operations were hampered by gunfire from shore batteries and by high seas, the latter causing a PBM rescue aircraft to crash. Eleven men were killed, seven of them from the P2V crew.

The Korean War, which came to an end on 27 July 1953 following the signing of an armistice agreement at Panmunjom, taught the western allies a great deal that would be applied to tactical and strategic planning in the years to come. One of the principal lessons was that far greater emphasis must be laid on the gathering of signals and electronic intelligence. The sophistication of the Soviet early warning and GCI radar systems supplied to the Chinese and North Koreans as the war progressed had come as an unpleasant surprise to the Americans, especially since those involved in developing a new generation of high-flying reconnaissance aircraft believed, in 1952, that the Russians were still using an air defence system based on American-designed radars supplied under lend-lease to the Soviet Union in the Second World War, and whose limitations were well known.

The growing Russian expertise in air defence radar development, the deployment of modern jet interceptors in large numbers, the launching of what appeared to be a long-range missile research and development programme in the USSR and the possession of nuclear weapons added up to a dangerous recipe whose secret ingredients could only be revealed by air reconnaissance on a hitherto unprecedented scale. The high cold war was just beginning.

5

RAF Strategic Intelligence Operations, 1946–54

AT THE END of the Second World War, the Royal Air Force had nine dedicated photographic reconnaissance squadrons on strength at home and abroad. One of the squadrons responsible for the coverage of northwest Europe, No. 542, disbanded soon after the war's end, and a second, No. 544, followed suit in October 1945. The two remaining squadrons in the theatre, No. 540, based at Benson in Oxfordshire and armed with Mosquito Mk 32s, and No. 541, with Spitfires and Mustangs, disbanded in September 1946. In the following month No. 58 Squadron reformed at Benson with Mosquito PR.34s and took over the UK-based reconnaissance task.

Overseas, No. 680 Squadron took its Mosquitos – also PR.34s – from Iraq to Palestine in September 1946 and was renumbered 13 Squadron, while No. 681 Squadron, redeployed from Singapore to India in May 1946 with Spitfire XIXs, was renumbered 34 Squadron in August. This squadron continued to fly Spitfires until July 1947, when it disbanded.

Nos 682 and 683 Squadrons, which had flown PR Spitfires in Italy and the Balkans, both disbanded in 1945, while No. 684 Squadron, armed with PR.34 Mosquitos and operating at various locations in South-East Asia, was renumbered 81 Squadron in September 1946. No. 81 was to remain the Far East Air Force's reconnaissance element for many years, and was heavily involved in Operation *Firedog*, the campaign against communist terrorism.

At the beginning of 1947, No. 58 Squadron was the sole UK-based PR unit, but this state of affairs was not to last for long. In November 1947 No. 541 Squadron was reformed, also at Benson, with Spitfire Mk XIXs in the tactical reconnaissance role, and the Benson establishment was augmented further in December, when No. 540 Squadron reformed with Mosquito PR.34s. In addition to these, the squadron received some PR.35s, equipped for night radar reconnaissance. Specialised training for the reconnaissance crews was undertaken by No. 8 Operational Training Unit, which became No. 237 OCU in July 1947.

All the crews assigned to the three squadrons were experienced, and during the next two years they carried out a number of high-altitude reconnaissance sorties over eastern Europe. Meanwhile, Mosquitos of No. 13 Squadron, deployed to Habbaniyah in Iraq, made penetrations of Soviet air space to photograph installations in the area of

An Israeli Air Force Spitfire LF.IX. Israeli Spitfires destroyed four RAF Spitfires and a Tempest carrying out armed reconnaissance missions during the Arab–Israeli War of 1948–49.

the Caspian Sea. All these flights were made without incident, but were discontinued late in 1948 with the first deployments of Russia's MiG-15 interceptor. No. 13 Squadron also carried out reconnaissance flights over Israel at the time of the 1948–49 Arab–Israeli War, but these too were stopped after Israeli Air Force Spitfires shot down four RAF Spitfires of No. 208 Squadron and a Tempest of No. 213 on armed reconnaissance missions over the combat zone.

The RAF, with unpleasant memories of the ease with which its PR aircraft had been intercepted by Messerschmitt 262 jet fighters in the closing months of the Second World War, was under no illusion about the chances of survival of piston-engined types in an environment dominated by jet interceptors, and the fact that its Mosquitos could no longer penetrate Soviet air space with impunity opened up a critical strategic reconnaissance gap that could only be filled when jet aircraft assumed the PR task.

The aircraft under development for this role was the PR version of the English Electric Canberra light jet bomber, but as we shall see in a later chapter its entry into service was delayed by various problems, and in the meantime some form of stop-gap aircraft was necessary.

The fact that jet aircraft promised to be effective in the high-altitude PR role was underlined when, on 23 March 1948, de Havilland test pilot John Cunningham attained a record altitude of 59,492 feet in a Vampire fitted with A Ghost turbojet engine and four-foot wing extensions; but a possible reconnaissance version of the Vampire was ruled out by the aircraft's limited range. The idea was resurrected at a later date, in

1952, when Cunningham and fellow test pilot John Wilson were asked to assess the Vampire's successor, the de Havilland Venom, as a potential high-altitude reconnaissance aircraft capable of making short penetrations over eastern Europe at altitudes in excess of 50,000 feet. Two aircraft (WE265 and WE275) were involved, and were stripped of all unnecessary equipment such as tip tanks, armament, armour plate and radios for the trials.

During the trials, the Venoms reached a maximum altitude of 52,500 feet, but at that height they were unstable and capable of only limited manoeuvres. One of the aircraft, WE275, was painted cerulean blue overall and deployed temporarily to either Wunstorf or Buckeburg, in Germany, but although some sources claim that it made several operational sorties over the eastern zone there is no evidence that it ever did.

In December 1950, meanwhile, No. 541 Squadron at Benson had begun to rearm with the Gloster Meteor PR.10, achieving a unit establishment of 14 aircraft by the following February. In June 1951 the Squadron deployed to Buckeburg as part of 2nd TAF. The PR.10 was fitted with the long-span wings of the Mk.3 fighter and was unarmed. Photographic equipment comprised an F.24 camera in the nose, which was controlled by the pilot and able to take oblique shots through two side and one nose panels, and two type F.52s in the ventral portion of the rear fuselage. These were also remotely controlled by the pilot by means of a Type 35 No. 8 controller positioned in the space normally occupied by the gyro gunsight, and were heated by air drawn from the port engine compressor casing.

The Meteor PR.10's operational ceiling was 47,000 feet and its endurance 3 hours 40 minutes with wing and ventral tanks. No. 541 Squadron used the type until its disbandment in September 1957, and during the early part of their six-year period of service the Meteors undertook numerous short-range penetration flights into eastern bloc air space, gathering target intelligence for 2nd TAF. These missions became too dangerous to sustain after the Soviet Air Force began to deploy MiG-19 supersonic interceptors to Eastern Germany in 1956, but the Meteors continued to fly reconnaissance sorties along the border.

On 15 July 1951, in response to the growing need to gather electronic intelligence, No. 192 Squadron was reformed at RAF Watton, Norfolk, and armed initially with Lincoln B.2 aircraft converted for the ELINT role. The Lincoln was not really suited to the task; although it had a substantial range, it was slow and lacked altitude performance (290 mph and 22,000 feet). In April 1952, therefore, No. 192 Squadron was allocated four RB-29As; these aircraft were part of a package of B-29s, 87 aircraft in all, supplied to the RAF under the Mutual Defense Assistance Program to fill the gap until the Canberra light bomber became operational. The B-29 was called the Washington in RAF service.

Bomber Command returned most of its surviving Washingtons – about a dozen having been scrapped or lost in accidents – to the United States in 1953–4, but No. 192 Squadron's aircraft remained in service in the ELINT role until 1958. In addition to monitoring land-based Russian radar and signals traffic during sorties flown mainly over the Baltic and the Black Sea, with occasional runs along Iran's border with the USSR and trips to Bodo in Norway to operate off North Russia, the Squadron also logged naval communications from Soviet warships. None of the four RB-29As was lost, although many interceptions by Soviet fighters were recorded, particularly over the sensitive area of the Black Sea.

No. 192 Squadron's missions were often dangerous; there were no guarantees that

North American B-45 Tornado using rocket assisted take-off gear (RATOG). The reconnaissance version, the RB-45C, made a series of overflights of the USSR manned by RAF crews.

the Washingtons would not be attacked by Russian fighter pilots. But during the early years of the 1950s a small group of RAF pilots, operating in conditions of the utmost secrecy, carried out a number of sorties that were perilous in the extreme, involving flights deep into western Soviet Union.

In July 1951, Squadron Leader John Crampton, then commanding No. 97 (Lincoln) Squadron at RAF Hemswell, was summoned to HQ Bomber Command at RAF High Wycombe to be told by the AOC-in-C, Air Chief Marshal Sir Hugh P. Lloyd, that he was to assume command of a Special Duty Flight whose operations would be conducted in conditions of utmost secrecy. The Flight would be equipped with the North American RB-45C, the reconnaissance version of America's first operational multijet bomber, and the aircrew involved – nine in all, including Crampton – were to assemble at RAF Sculthorpe in Norfolk, one of the UK bases used by Strategic Air Command, before proceeding to the USA for a 60-day period of training. On 3 August 1951 the RAF personnel flew to Barksdale AFB, Louisiana, and spent ten days familiarising themselves with the B-45 bomber before flying to Lockbourne AFB, Ohio, to become acquainted with the RB-45C variant. Lockbourne was the home base of the three RB-45C squadrons of the 91st Strategic Reconnaissance Wing; two were absent on overseas deployments and the RAF crews converted with the 323rd SRS.

One of the RAF pilots was returned to the UK after writing off an aircraft in a heavy

RAF RB-45C flights over the USSR were supported by Boeing KB-29M flight refuelling tankers.

night landing, luckily with no damage to his crew, and his place was taken by another RAF pilot already on secondment to a B-45 squadron. After successfully completing their conversion course, the crews returned to Sculthorpe and were attached to the RB-45C unit already in residence there. Neither the British nor their American hosts had any inkling about what was in the offing, and it was not until early 1952 that Sqn Ldr Crampton and his navigator, Flt Lt Rex Sanders, were summoned to Bomber Command HQ to be told about their mission, which was to carry out night radar photography of routes over which RAF and USAF bombers would fly to targets in the Baltic States, the Moscow area and Central Southern Russia. One of the principal concerns was to detect surface-to-air missile (SAM) sites (the Russians were known to be developing a SAM system, although in fact this, based on the SA-1 *Guild*, would not be operational until at least 1954) and to try to establish evidence of the deployment of surface-to-surface missiles.

Four RB-45Cs (three operational aircraft and one spare) were allocated to the Special Duty flight; these were stripped of all USAF markings at RAF West Raynham and repainted in RAF insignia before returning to Sculthorpe. Before the first mission, Sq Ldr Crampton and his crew made a 30-minute flight over the Soviet Zone of Germany while ground stations listened for unusual Russian radio and radar activity that might indicate the flight was being tracked, but nothing untoward was noted and it was decided to proceed with the principal mission.

All three routes were to be flown simultaneously, the three aircraft departing Sculthorpe in rapid succession and heading for a point north of Denmark, where they were to make rendezvous with USAF KB-29 tankers. After taking on the maximum possible fuel load they were to climb at maximum continuous power at 0.68M until they reached the highest attainable altitude the prevailing conditions would permit. As they made their penetrations, the intelligence agencies would again be listening for signs of a Russian reaction. Radio silence would be broken only in the direst emergency. When the crews were briefed they received three separate weather forecasts for each route: a genuine one and two bogus ones. One of the latter was to uphold their Sculthorpe 'cover story' and the other was for the benefit of Russian interrogators if they were forced down and captured; the crews were to maintain that they had been involved in a weather reconnaissance of the Black Sea in the case of the southern route and of the Gulf of Bothnia in the case of the northern ones, and that they had strayed off course.

The first sortie was flown in April 1952, the aircraft taking off from Sculthorpe in the late afternoon. The three crews were: Sqn Ldr John Crampton, Flt Lt Rex Sanders and Sgt Lindsay; Flt Lt Gordon Cremer, Flt Sgt Bob Anstee and Sgt Don Greenslade; Flt Lt Bill Blair, Flt Lt John Hill and Flt Sgt Joe Acklam.

The aircraft made rendezvous with their tankers and then headed into Soviet air space, all lights extinguished. Sqn Ldr Crampton's crew had the longest haul, south-east across Russia, and he later recalled that his most enduring memory of the route was the apparent wilderness over which he was flying. There were no lights on the ground and no apparent sign of human habitation, a scene quite different from the rest of Europe.

All the target photographs were taken as planned, the navigators taking 35 mm photographs of the radar displays, and all three aircraft returned to base safely, though not without incident; about 20 minutes before the first aircraft (Flt Lt Blair) was due to arrive at Sculthorpe low stratus started to roll in from the North Sea, so he had to divert to Manston. Sqn Ldr Crampton arrived during a temporary break in the weather and got in successfully, but Flt Lt Cremer, who had had to land at Copenhagen because of iced-up fuel filters, had to divert into Prestwick.

A few days later the RB-45Cs, still bearing RAF markings, were returned to Lockbourne AFB and the crews returned to other duties, Sqn Ldr Crampton being given command of No. 101 Squadron at Binbrook, the first to rearm with Canberras. In October 1952 the Special Duty Flight was reactivated, again with RB-45Cs and with Crampton in command, but with a couple of changes of personnel. His previous co-pilot, Sgt Lindsay, had been involved in a B-29 crash and his place was taken by Flt Lt McAlistair Furze, a flight commander on No. 101 Squadron, known to all and sundry as 'McFurze'. The crews embarked on a period of intensive training, only to have the forthcoming operation cancelled early in December.

The Special Duty Flight was again activated in March 1954. Again the crews were briefed to cover three routes, north, central and southern; the latter was a long and potentially dangerous trip that would require refuelling inbound as well as outbound, and Sqn Ldr Crampton selected this one for himself. There was some comfort to be derived from the Intelligence briefing, at which he had been told that although his aircraft might be tracked by Soviet GCI, he was not likely to encounter radar-equipped night-fighters and he need not worry about flak, as he would be flying too high and too fast.

Late in April, the three RB-45Cs once again refuelled off northern Denmark and set off on their respective routes. Apart from the replacement of Sgt Lindsay by Flt Lt Furze, already mentioned, the other crew change was in Crew 3, where Flt Lt Bill Blair was replaced by Flt Lt Harry Currell.

The first leg of Sqn Ldr Crampton's flight took him towards Kiev, and as he flew on at 36,000 feet and a steady 0.7M he noticed what looked like lightning flashes twinkling on the ground far below. Then, as he approached Kiev, the sky ahead erupted with what he later described as a 'veritable flare path of exploding golden anti-aircraft fire', at the same height as the RB-45C and a few hundred yards in front. His reaction was instinctive; he pushed the throttles wide open and turned west, heading for Germany, a good 1,000 miles away. His destination was Furstenfeldbruck, the planned air refuelling rendezvous and emergency alternative airfield.

Contact was made with the KB-29 tanker as scheduled, but because of a refuelling malfunction Crampton decided to land at Furstenfeldbruck and top up there before returning to Sculthorpe, where the other two aircraft had already landed. Their flights had been without incident, but the results obtained on this mission were analysed as only partially successful. It is quite possible that the operation was compromised; for a year beforehand, letters had been appearing in various UK aviation publications, questioning the presence at Sculthorpe of mysterious RB-45Cs bearing RAF markings, and the British Intelligence system itself – although this was not known at the time – had been infiltrated at senior levels by communist sympathisers.

In fact, the intelligence material gathered during the whole series of overflights was far less than had been hoped or anticipated. At best, the flights had given a small number of RAF crews experience of high-altitude reconnaissance operations over hostile territory. In vew of the fact that on 16 December 1952, after a thorough analysis of the early flights, Air Chief Marshal Sir Hugh P. Lloyd had written to Major-General John P. McConnell, commanding the British-based USAF 7th Air Division, and expressed his regrets that the operation had not provided the required answers, it is surprising that the second series of flights had been authorised at all.

That they were was indicative of the desperate need that now attended the requirement to obtain strategic intelligence of the Soviet Union and its defences. The Americans, labouring under political constraints since the destruction of the Privateer ELINT aircraft over the Baltic in 1950, were unable to achieve their intelligence goals, and were prompted to offer the loan of the RB-45Cs (via the USAF Chief of Staff, General Hoyt S. Vandenberg) to the RAF on the 'gentleman's understanding' that any photographic intelligence obtained by them would be jointly shared. In the meantime, the USAF was restricted to ELINT flights around the periphery of the Soviet Union; and these flights served only to underline the growing might of Soviet air power in a world increasingly dominated by nuclear confrontation.

6

USAF ELINT Operations, 1950–54

THE EXPANSION OF Strategic Air Command's reconnaissance assets had really got under way in the summer of 1950 with the delivery of three new aircraft types, beginning with the Convair RB-36D. This strategic reconnaissance version of the massive global bomber had 14 cameras weighing 3,309 lb in the forward bomb bay, the second bay containing up to 80 T86 flash bulbs. An extra 3,000-gallon fuel tank could be installed in the third bay, and ECM equipment in the fourth. The RB-36D carried standard gun armament, together with an AN/APQ-24 radar navigation system for locating targets. The aircraft carried a crew of 18, later rising to 22 with the addition of four more specialist crewmen.

The Boeing RB-50 entered USAF service in July 1950.

Incursions by American reconnaissance aircraft led to the Russians accelerating their night-fighter development programme. The Lavochkin La-200 and the MiG I-320R were two unsuccessful contenders.

The first RB-36D (44-92091) was delivered on 2 June 1950 to the 28th Strategic Reconnaissance Wing at Rapid City AFB, South Dakota, which became operational in the following year. In December 1950 the 5th SRW at Travis AFB also began to rearm with the RB-36D, the establishment of the two wings being 18 and 22 aircraft respectively. In fact only 31 RB-36Ds were built, so re-equipment of the 5th SRW was completed with the RB-36E version. This was a converted B-36A, and the last of 22 examples was delivered in July 1951.

The next strategic reconnaissance aircraft was the RB-50B, the first of which (47-123) was delivered to the 91st SRW at Barksdale AFB, Louisiana, on 12 July 1950. A few weeks later, on 26 August, the 91st SRW also took delivery of its first RB-45C. From April 1951 the RB-50Bs were redesignated according to their specific tasks: RB-50E for photographic reconnaissance, RB-50F for photo-mapping, and RB-50G for electronic reconnaissance.

From 1951 overflights of Soviet arctic bases were made by RB-36s operating from British bases, mostly Sculthorpe, the main area of interest being the island of Novaya Zemlya, where the Russians were building what appeared to be a large nuclear weapons test complex. (It was; most Russian nuclear testing took place there from 1958 to 1964.) These excursions resulted, in November 1951, in the Soviet Aviation Ministry issuing an urgent specification for an all-weather fighter fitted with a long-range search radar, the *Izumrud* (Emerald) AI radar then carried by existing Soviet fighter types being quite inadequate for the interception of the American reconnaissance aircraft. It was not until 1956 that such an aircraft – the Yakovlev Yak-25 Flashlight – entered service with the Soviet Air Force's fighter squadrons, and until then the reconnaissance flights were continued with impunity.

Meanwhile, RB-50s and RB-45Cs were flying 'ferret' missions over the Soviet Union, their task becoming more urgent when the Russians exploded their second atomic bomb (*Joe 2*) at the Central Asian test site on 24 September 1951. This test used plutonium as the fissionable material, and the intensity of the acoustic signals picked up by ground and airborne stations was about the same magnitude as those associated with the American 'Greenhouse' series of tests in the Pacific in April and May that year. The Russians, it appeared, were catching up.

Successful ferret missions depended on locating gaps, or 'dead spots' in the Russian radar defences, which was done initially by monitoring Soviet radio and radar traffic from ground stations in Europe, the Middle East and Far East. When such a dead spot was found, a penetration of some 25 or 30 miles would be made – often longer in the case of eastern and southern areas, where radar coverage was poorer – the ferret aircraft staging out of bases such as Rhein-Main in Germany, Mildenhall, Lakenheath and Sculthorpe in the United Kingdom, Atsugi, Misawa and Iwakuni in Japan, Kadena on Okinawa, Sangley Point in the Philippines, and other locations in Norway and Libya.

Ferret crews were left under no illusions by their briefing officers about their chances of being rescued if they were forced down in hostile territory. There was none. Their only hope of survival, if they sighted enemy fighters, was to find a cloud formation large enough to conceal them before they were intercepted. Clear skies were anathema to them, and yet many operations were flown in clear weather. It was quite amazing that no USAF aircraft was shot down over the Soviet Union during this dangerous period of the early 1950s.

By the end of 1953 SAC had four heavy strategic reconnaissance wings, the 5th, 28th, 72nd and 99th, all equipped with the RB-36. The earlier RB-36D/Es had now

Initial development of the 'parasite' fighter/reconnaissance aircraft concept was carried out by the McDonnell XF-85 Goblin.

been joined by two later versions, the RB-36F and the RB-36H, both of which featured modifications and updates in parallel with those of the bombers from which they were derived. Twenty-four RB-36Fs were delivered, and 73 RB-36Hs.

In 1951, one of the RB-36Fs, 49-2707, was assigned to the FICON (Fighter Conveyor) programme, resurrected from an earlier unsuccessful programme involving the McDonnell XF-85 'parasite' fighter. The plan was to use the B-36 to carry an F-84E Thunderjet, and the modified trials aircraft, now designated GRB-36F, made its first contact flight with the fighter on 9 January 1952. This was followed, on 23 April, by the first in-flight retrieval and launch of an F-84E, and on 14 May the first composite flight was made with the Thunderjet positioned in the bomb bay during take-off and landing.

By 20 February 1953 the composite GRB-36F/F-84E had completed 170 airborne launches and retrievals, paving the way for further trials with a swept-wing F-84F Thunderstreak. The idea now was that the B-36 could be used to carry an RF-84F Thunderflash reconnaissance fighter; the latter would be launched at some point outside hostile territory, up to 2,800 miles from the B-36's base, at an altitude of 25,000 feet and would then fly 1,180 miles to make a dash over the target at high speed (580 mph at 35,000 feet or 630 mph at sea level), after which it would be retrieved by the parent aircraft. It was a desperate idea born of desperate times.

Opposite and above: *A Republic YRF-84F Thunderflash hooks up to its parent GRB-36F during FICON trials. Production RF-84Fs had wing root air intakes.*

An RF-84F is recessed into a GRB-36F. During trials, most RF-84s were loaded into the parent aircraft following a mid-air link-up.

An RF-84F linked to the wingtip of an RB-36 during Project Tom-Tom *trials.*

In May 1953, contracts were awarded to Convair and Republic for the modification of ten B-36Ds into carrier aircraft and 25 RF-84s as parasites, the types being re-designated GRB-36D and RF-64K. The latter weighed 29,503 lb and was armed with five cameras and four 0.5-inch machine guns. The GRB-36D retained its cameras and tail armament, all other defensive weapons being deleted, and its ECM equipment was moved aft to make room for bomb bay installation of an H-shaped cradle that was lowered to launch or retrieve the RF-84K. The Thunderflash could be refuelled in the bomb bay, and the pilot was able to leave the cockpit if necessary.

In December 1954 the 91st Strategic Reconnaissance Squadron (Fighter) was activated and attached to the 407th Strategic Fighter Wing at Great Falls AFB, the pilots being trained on standard F-84F Thunderstreaks. On 24 January 1955 the 71st SRW (F) was activated at Larson AFB, Washington, with two squadrons (the 25th and 82nd SRS (F)) of basic RF-84Fs, and the 91st SRS joined them there with its RF-84Ks in July. Meanwhile, the modified GRB-36Ds were being delivered to the 99th SRW at Fairchild AFB, which was nearby, and operational training between the two units was under way by the end of the year. The system presented continual difficulties however, and the partnership lasted less than a year, the 91st SRS (F) exchanging its RF-84Ks for RF-84Fs late in 1956. It remained part of the 71st SRW (F) until the latter was deactivated on 1 July 1957.

Opposite: *The Boeing RB-47 Stratojet brought a new dimension to strategic reconnaissance, and gave excellent service throughout the most dangerous years of the Cold War. Illustrated is an RB-47H of the 55th SRW at RAF Upper Heyford.*

In 1952–3, parasite fighter trials were also carried out in connection with Project *Tom-Tom*, a concept that involved two F-84F fighters hooking up to an assembly fitted to a B-36's wingtips. This also started life as a fighter conveyor project, but was subsequently adapted to the strategic reconnaissance role. The aircraft used in these trials were RB-36F 49-2707 and RF-84Fs 51-1848 and 51-1849. Modifications included podded, articulated arm assemblies on the RB-36F and articulated jaw-like clamps on the RF-84Fs, to hold the fighters in position. The first hook-up was made early in 1953, using only one RF-84F, after a series of trials to determine the best approach methods. Several more hook-ups were made subsequently, but because of the enormous slipstream and wingtip vortices generated by the RB-36 the operation was extremely dangerous. The programme was terminated late in 1953 after severe oscillation caused an RF-84F to tear loose from the parent aircraft's hook-up arm.

In any case, by this time the advent of new, high-speed jet reconnaissance aircraft had done away with the need to adopt such drastic stop-gap measures. It was in 1953 that SAC began to receive the first reconnaissance version of the Boeing B-47 Stratojet. The first new-build variant that was specifically dedicated to the reconnaissance role was the RB-47E, but delays in production during 1952 led to the choice of an interim conversion. Camera pods were fitted to 90 B-47Bs, which were then designated YRB-47B. In fact, the first batch of YRB-47Bs, minus reconnaissance equipment, was delivered to the 20th Bomb Wing at Mather AFB for use in bombardment training, and it was not until 25 April 1953 that the first YRB-47B with its full eight-camera bomb bay pod was delivered to the 91st SRW at Lockbourne AFB. In September the 26th SRW, also at Lockbourne, became the second unit to arm with the YRB-47B.

Both wings began to re-equip with the RB-47E during 1954, two more units also receiving this variant in the course of the year. These were the 55th SRW, a former RB-50 unit, and the 90th SRW, which had operated RB-29s. Both were located at Forbes AFB, Kansas. The fifth and last unit to equip with the RB-47E was the 70th SRW, which was activated at Little Rock AFB in 1955. In all, 240 RB-47Es were delivered to SAC.

Two more reconnaissance variants of the Stratojet were produced. These were the RB-47H and RB-47K, which were modified for the ELINT role and had a pressurised compartment containing three electronics warfare specialists in the bomb bay. Thirty-five RB-47Hs and 15 RB-47Ks were built, the former being delivered to the 38th and 346th SRS and the latter to the 338th SRS of the 55th SRW in 1955–56.

In the RB-47H the specialist signals operators – known popularly as 'Crows', although officially called Ravens – were crammed into a compartment only four feet high, forcing them to move about on their knees. All three Crows had to cram themselves into the cockpit before take-off, then crawl down into the compartment, where they sat facing aft, strapped into ejection seats and with solid banks of equipment – scopes, analysers, receivers, recorders and controls – in front and on one side.

Raven One was the commander and sat in the right forward corner of the compartment. As well as the banks of equipment in front of him and on his left, there was an array of video, digital and analog recorders along the wall to his right and behind him. Ravens Two and Three sat side by side at the rear of the compartment, with just enough room between their seats for someone to squeeze through.

On the day before a sortie into a sensitive area, specialist crews were given a very comprehensive briefing covering the route, timing, up-to-date intelligence on likely defences, and specific tasking. To perform a mission successfully required a great deal of experience, but a Crow who was good at his job could identify an intercepted signal from its various characteristics – frequency, pulse shape, pulse rate, type of modulation, type of scan and so on – displayed on his equipment. These functions determined the radar's function, be it early warning, search or fire control. Variations were what the specialists were seeking; emitters were constantly being modified to increase their capability or to defeat surveillance and countermeasures techniques.

At a predetermined point during the mission the Crows began processing signals, keeping each other constantly informed about activity on their assigned bands. If, for example, an SA-2 surface-to-air missile radar was activated, one Crow would track it while another looked for the missile guidance signal. It was difficult work, for there might be a couple of dozen signals in the narrow band to which each receiver was tuned. As well as audio recordings, signals appearing on oscilloscopes and other visual equipment were filmed and photographed. By switching to one of the direction-finding antennae, which rotated at 300 rpm, the Crows could log a number of bearings to obtain a position fix on a transmitter.

On some sorties, RB-47 crews logged several interceptions by Soviet fighters; detecting their approach was the responsibility of Raven One, who would identify the aircraft from the signals emitted by their AI radars and weapon systems and alert the pilots to their presence. Sometimes, if the Russians showed signs of aggression, the mission had to be aborted and Raven One used chaff and jammers while the RB-47 got clear of the danger area. Often, however, flights were long and boring, with no sign of activity. 'Those sorties,' one former Crow recalled, 'gave us time to dream up pranks. Since a Crow's greatest ambition was to pick up a new or unusual signal, we sometimes made up our own. We brought kazoos, noise makers, Japanese battery-operated toys, whistles, signal generators, and other devices to stump the analysts. Once we brought a cricket along and recorded its chirping, which we mixed with the navigation radar pulse and electrical noise from a fuel boost pump. We recorded and photographed the result and called it a new signal, speculating that it was most likely from an advanced fighter radar. Two weeks later the analysts' report came back. They had properly identified the nav radar, the boost pump, and the cricket. As a crowning blow, they had even determined the cabin temperature at the time of the recording and the sex of the cricket.'

Despite such diversions, the ferret crews were under no illusion about the serious nature of their missions. Even though overflights were still banned in the mid-1950s, flights along the frontiers of the Soviet Union were dangerous enough, and Soviet air defence technology was becoming increasingly sophisticated. In the face of the American strategic threat, Soviet planners had given a very high priority to the creation of an effective air defence system in the late 1940s, which in practice meant the co-ordinated development of jet interceptors, anti-aircraft artillery and radar networks, with surface-to-air missile deployment envisaged in the not too distant future. These elements were the responsibility of the Air Defence Command, the *Protivo-Vozdushnaya Oborona* (PVO), which was rapidly bringing new aircraft types into its inventory. By the end of 1952 the successor to the well-tried and combat-proven MiG-15, the MiG-17 (NATO reporting name *Fresco*) had completed its State Acceptance Trials and the type went into production immediately, entering service in 1953. The *Fresco*-B, or MiG-17P (P for *Poiskoviy*, meaning search radar) was equipped with the *Izumrud* AI kit; the *Fresco*-C, or MiG-17F (*Forsazh*, meaning afterburner) was fitted with reheat, boosting the performance of its Klimov VK-1 engine to 7,500 lb; and a later model, the MiG-17PF *Fresco*-D, was equipped, as its suffix denoted, with both AI radar and afterburner.

The *Fresco*, as RB-47 crews soon learned, had a performance that matched that of their own aircraft, which was now outstripped in terms of both maximum speed and operational ceiling. This fact had serious implications for Strategic Air Command's main striking force, which in 1953 was in the process of re-arming with the B-47. The ability of the B-47 to penetrate Russia's air defences was in serious doubt, and on 8 May 1954 the Americans felt justified in taking an appalling risk by sending an RB-47 of the 91st SRW on a photographic mission over the northern USSR, with fighter airfields as its main objectives. The flight appears to have been authorised by General Curtis LeMay, SAC's commander; in all probability, neither the State Department nor President Eisenhower had any knowledge of it.

The RB-47, which took off from RAF Fairford in Gloucestershire, was supported by two others, which flew a feint mission towards the Kola peninsula before turning back, leaving the photographic aircraft to penetrate in the Murmansk area and continue to Archangel'sk before turning south-west to fly over Finland, the Gulf of Bothnia and Sweden before making a timely refuelling rendezvous with a KC-97 tanker over Norway. The RB-47 was intercepted by MiG-17s and took some hits, but at the altitude at which the interceptions took place the MiGs's cannon recoil gave them some stability problems and they were unable to sustain their attacks. The RB-47 crew replied with their twin 20 mm tail cannon, which helped to keep the MiGs at bay, but they were extremely lucky to get away with it.

The Kola mission showed that, once again, the Americans had a strategic reconnaissance gap to fill, and it could not have opened up at a worse time. On 12 August 1953, the Russians exploded their first thermonuclear device, and before the end of the year they had tested three more, at least one of which was thought to be an air drop. The Americans had to assume that the Russians had already deployed operational atomic bombs (in fact, they were only just doing so in late 1953) and were on the verge of deploying operational thermonuclear weapons. Constant surveillance of nuclear test sites, bomber airfields and missile development centres was now no longer just a question of strategic importance; it was a question of survival. And it was at this juncture that the Royal Air Force stepped in to help fill the reconnaissance void.

7

RAF Canberra PR and ELINT Missions: The UK Squadrons

THE CANBERRA'S ROLE as a photographic reconnaissance aircraft, one of the most important it was to fulfil over the years, was dictated by specification PR31/46, which in effect called for a PR version of the B.5/47 Canberra B.2. The main external difference between the B.2 and the PR variant, designated PR.Mk.3, was that the latter's front fuselage was extended by 14 inches to accommodate a 415-gallon ventral fuel tank, a camera bay and a flare bay. For the day photography role the PR.3 was equipped with either four or six F.52 and one F.49 cameras, while equipment for the night role comprised two F.89 cameras, photocells and a 1.75 photoflash crate. The aircraft carried a crew of two.

The prototype PR.3, VX181, was flown for the first time from Samlesbury on 19 March 1950, but during subsequent test flying severe vibration problems – caused by

Canberra VN813, the second prototype, was fitted with a de Havilland Spectre rocket motor for extra high-altitude performance.

Fitted with a Scorpion rocket motor, the Canberra B.2 might have been a contender for the high-altitude reconnaissance role. The aircraft pictured, WK163, established a World Altitude Record of 71,310 feet on 28 August 1957 and was used for nuclear cloud sampling.

the fuselage extension and consequent redistribution of mass – were encountered, and a speed restriction of 0.75M was placed on the aircraft (compared with 0.84M for the B.2). The problem was eventually alleviated by increasing the elevator and tab mass balances, but it was never cured completely.

All this delayed the PR.3's CA (Comptroller Aircraft) Release, and it was not until 31 July 1952 that the first of an initial production batch of 27 aircraft, WE135, took to the air. It was allocated to No. 540 Squadron at Benson for operational trials, and re-equipment of this unit with the PR.3 began in December. WE135 then went to the PR element of No. 231 OCU, the Canberra operational conversion unit.

In March 1953 No. 540 Squadron moved to RAF Wyton, near Huntingdon, together with Nos 58 and 82 Squadrons. The latter began to re-equip with Canberra PR.3s in November 1953 and No. 58 Squadron followed soon afterwards, using Canberras re-allocated from the other two units.

In the meantime, an RAF Canberra had become the focus of a rather odd story, one which remains uncorroborated to this day. It first came to light in a book, published in 1968, about the activities of the Central Intelligence Agency (*The Centre*, Steward

Alsop, New York: Popular Library p.194) in which it was stated that a modified Mk 2 Canberra 'flew at its maximum altitude from a base in West Germany, photographed the missile launch site at Kapustin Yar in the Soviet Union, and landed at a base in Iran. The Soviets – possibly forewarned by Kim Philby, the life-long Soviet spy then in charge of British intelligence's anti-Soviet operations – very nearly succeeded in shooting down the Canberra, which took several hits.'

The background to this story is that towards the end of 1952 the CIA became aware, through interrogation of German scientists and other personnel who were slowly being repatriated from the Soviet Union, that a missile test facility had been set up at Kapustin Yar, north of the Caspian Sea (48 35N, 46 18E). In fact, testing had been in progress there since 1947, with the launching of captured German V-2 rockets and derivatives of them. The first Soviet serial production version of the V-2 was known to NATO as the SS-1a *Scunner*, which was followed, in 1950, by a longer-range variant, the SS-2 *Sibling*. Neither of these weapons was deployed operationally, and at the end of 1952 there were indications that the emphasis was shifting towards the development of surface-to-air missiles and very long range strategic rockets.

It therefore became a matter of the highest priority to establish exactly what was going on at Kapustin Yar, and that meant clandestine photo reconnaissance. Robert Amory, Jr, who at that time was the CIA's deputy director for intelligence, later stated in an Oral History interview that the CIA requested photographic coverage of the site, but was told by General Nathan F. Twining, the US Air Force Chief of Staff, that Kapustin Yar was outside effective reconnaissance range (in other words, it was beyond the range of any camera operating outside Soviet air space, as overflights were still vetoed) and that the USAF could not undertake the mission.

One of the RAF's PR Canberras, however, was capable of making a daylight sortie to Kapustin Yar, and the subsequent scenario is as follows. The CIA, presumably through clandestine diplomatic channels (which probably meant the Secret Intelligence Service) approached the RAF and asked them to do the job. A Canberra was specially modified with a 100-inch focal length camera of American design and provided with extra fuel tankage, and sometime in the early summer of 1953 it took off from Giebelstadt in Germany, flew over eastern Europe at altitude, turned south along the Volga to Kapustin Yar, and landed in Iran. Somewhere along its route it was intercepted, shot at, and damaged.

Out of all the fog that surrounds this operation, which was given the code-name *Robin*, one fact appears to emerge. The aircraft was not a Canberra PR.3, but a B.2 specially modified for the job. One of the keenest researchers into the mystery, investigative reporter and television producer Paul Lashmar, believes that it was WH726, the only B.2 allocated to No. 540 (PR) Squadron. Other researchers think it might have been WD952, the Olympus-engined Canberra which had reached a record altitude of 63,668 feet on 4 May 1953, but Lashmar's theory seems more plausible. WH726 subsequently served with No. 58 (PR) Squadron and was sold to Peru in September 1966 as a B.72.

Whatever the truth, WH726 certainly flew other *Robin* sorties during its PR career, although of less dramatic nature. In 1954–55 Nos 58 and 540 Squadrons made frequent deployments to locations in the Middle East to carry out photographic sorties over the Soviet Black Sea ports and the Caucasus, although such penetrations were flown by only the most experienced crews and required authorisation at the highest level. The majority of sorties were flown at a distance of twelve miles or more from Soviet

Canberra PR.7 WH793 was used for unspecified duties with the Ministry of Supply and later became the PR.9 prototype.

territory, but at altitudes of 47,000 feet or more such missions could still yield substantial photographic intelligence.

Meanwhile, English Electric had developed a second Canberra photo-reconnaissance variant, the PR.7, which was similar to the PR.3 except that it had more powerful Rolls-Royce Avon RA.7 engines, wing leading edge fuel tanks and Maxaret anti-skid brakes. The PR.7 was to remain the workhorse of the Canberra PR fleet throughout its existence. As most of the modifications embodied in this mark had been cleared in VX185, which had been started as the second prototype Canberra PR.3 but completed as the Canberra B.5 (the only example of this mark to be built), there was no prototype PR.7; the first production aircraft, WH773, flew on 16 August 1953 and subsequently went to No. 540 Squadron. However, the first squadron to equip fully with the PR.7 was No. 542, the former PR Spitfire unit which reformed at Wyton on 17 May 1954. No. 542 Squadron's career as a PR Canberra unit was relatively short; it disbanded on 1 October 1955, to reform a month later for special operations in connection with the British nuclear weapons test programme.

By the end of 1954 Nos 82 and 540 Squadrons were both armed with the Canberra PR.7, but No. 58 Squadron was to retain its PR.3s until December 1955, when it too began to replace them with PR.7s. By this time, Bomber Command's reconnaissance capability had received an important boost in the shape of No. 543 (Strategic Reconnaissance) Squadron, which had reformed at Gaydon in July 1955 with Vickers Valiant B(PR) 1 aircraft and moved to Wyton in November; the main photographic task, however, remained with the Canberra squadrons. In March 1956 No. 540 Squadron disbanded, followed by No. 82 Squadron in September, leaving No. 58 Squadron as the sole PR Canberra squadron in the United Kingdom. From now on, its activities, alongside those of No. 543 Squadron, were closely linked to the operations of the

Infrared reconnaissance photograph of an airfield. Note the dark areas on the Canberra at lower left centre, denoting that it has been standing in the sun and its skin is warm. Its thermal shadow indicates that it has just been turned around; this fact, and servicing vehicles nearby, indicate that it is being prepared for take-off. The other aircraft, by way of contrast, has recently returned from a high level sortie; its skin is cool and only the engines show heat.

These photographs of 2 ATAF reconnaissance Canberras at low level clearly show the value of camouflage. The lower picture shows a Canberra flying over an earthquake-damaged town.

Getting into the bomb-aimer's/camera operator's position in a Canberra could be hard work, as this photograph of the narrow entrance to the nose position indicates.

V-Force, the RAF's strategic deterrent, although both units had the secondary task of undertaking photographic surveys on behalf of various Ministry departments and, on request, Commonwealth countries. Work carried out in the V-Force context included the photo-mapping of likely approach routes that would be flown by the V-bombers en route to their targets in hostile territory, and also the continuing updating of the charts used by the V-Force. This task became particularly important in the early 1960s with the introduction of the Blue Steel stand-off missile, whose inertial navigation system relied on very accurate position fixing during the run-up to weapon release.

Most of the training flights undertaken by No. 58 Squadron were by single aircraft, flying 'Lone Ranger' sorties to El Adem in Libya, Cyprus, Nairobi and the Persian Gulf. Frequent sorties were also made to the 2nd Tactical Air Force operational area; typically, a Canberra PR.7 would fly at high level to a point off the north coast of Germany, followed by a letdown into the recognised 2nd TAF low-level routes and a landing on a German airfield. On the way back to the UK from Germany a similar profile was used, the Canberra flying at high level and then descending to make use of the UK low-level routes. Sometimes the PR Canberras, operating from Bodo or Andoya in Norway, ventured deep inside the Arctic Circle; one of the longest of such missions, in December 1960, involved an overflight of Jan Mayen Island, 500 miles north north-east of Iceland.

A Canberra PR.9 showing the hinged nose access door. The navigator, who had no ejection seat, entered the aircraft through the nose section.

This flight was carried out by a Canberra PR.9, to which No. 58 Squadron began to convert early in 1960. The Canberra HA (High Altitude) PR.9 resulted from a contract awarded to English Electric in 1953 for a PR.7 development fitted with 11,250 lbst Avon RA.24 (Mk 206) engines which would, it was hoped, give it an operational ceiling in excess of 60,000 feet. The wing area was extended by a four-foot increase in the wing span and a large increase in the chord at the centre section between the engine nacelles and fuselage, which was designed to improve the compressibility boundary by reducing the thickness/chord ratio. Following initial design work at Warton, Napiers at Luton were sub-contracted to modify PR.7 WH793 as a prototype for the engine and wing modifications, and with these incorporated the aircraft flew from Cranfield on 8 July 1955.

Subsequent flight testing soon revealed that the PR.9's altitude performance fell short of expectations. Although the Mk 206 engines gave a good rate of climb to 50,000 feet it fell off rapidly above that altitude, and further tests revealed that induced drag from the new wing centre section at high altitude was virtually cancelling out the increased thrust margin. On 18 September 1956 test pilot Roland Beamont reached 59,000 feet in a PR.9, but the aircraft would go no higher and it had used a great deal of fuel in getting there.

Nevertheless, the altitude performance over that of the PR.7 was assessed as being sufficiently improved for the PR.9 to go into production, and two contracts were placed with the English Electric Company covering the manufacture of 24 aircraft. The first of these, XH129, flew on 27 July 1958 and was the first of the line to have a revised nose design, similar to that of the B(I)8 intruder version but with an upwards-opening pilot's canopy (which proved a boon when operating in hot climates). Entry to the navigator's compartment was also simplified by a sideways-opening nose section; beginning with the second production aircraft, the navigator was also provided with an ejection seat.

Canberra XH129's test programme was trouble-free until the final test, involving 5g manoeuvres at design IAS, before the aircraft went for evaluation at Boscombe Down. During this flight, on 9 October 1958, the aircraft went ito an uncontrollable roll to starboard, followed by a steep spiral dive. Project test pilot Don Knight managed to eject moments before the aircraft impacted in Liverpool Bay, but his observer was killed. The wreckage was recovered and the cause traced to the failure of the leading edge wing root skin attachments, which was attributed to the flexing of the enlarged wing section under extreme g loading. Modifications were carried out to aircraft on the production line and the first of these, XH136, was successfully tested by Roland Beamont on 20 January 1960.

By April 1960 three PR.9s, XH134, XH135 and XH136, had been delivered to No. 58 Squadron at Wyton; at this time the squadron still had thirteen PR.7s. During May and June, the PR.7s were used for trials in conjunction with No. 543 Squadron on shipping reconnaissance; in these, a Valiant of No. 543 Squadron was used as a high-level search aircraft, which vectored a Canberra on to a ship target. After descending to photograph the vessel the Canberra climbed to high level once more. These trials proved very successful and paved the way for later maritime radar reconnaissance techniques.

In July 1960 No. 58 Squadron had six PR.9s on strength, and now embarked on a period of intensive flying, with sorties flown at high and low level in an attempt to prove the fuel consumption graphs which had been compiled by the squadron from

This view of the prototype Canberra PR.9, WH793, clearly depicts the modified wing planform intended to enhance high-altitude performance – which in the event proved a disappointment.

data supplied by the Ministry of Aviation. Two of the low-level sorties were flown at a maximum speed of 360 knots, which was well in excess of the 250 kt limiting low-level speed which, until recently, had been the maximum permitted by Bomber Command. No particular problems were encountered, except that it was found impossible for the navigator to use the reconnaissance sight because of low-level turbulence.

The aircrews were impressed with the PR.9, and in particular with its rate of climb; it could reach 30,000 feet in two and a half minutes. High-level operation meant the use of partial pressure helmets and jerkins, and PR crews had to attend a course on the theory of high-altitude flight and its effects on the human body at the RAF Aeromedical Centre at Upwood, where they were subjected to simulated high altitude explosive decompression.

No. 58 Squadron was destined not to have a long period of operations with its PR.9s. There was a period of intense activity in October 1962, when these aircraft were used to photograph the movements of Soviet shipping en route to Cuba via the North Atlantic during the brief Missile Crisis, but after that the Squadron was gradually run down until disbandment in March 1963. Its Canberras were handed over early in 1963 to No. 39 Squadron, which continued to operate out of Luqa, Malta until September 1970, when it returned to the United Kingdom to become established at RAF Wyton. It operated the PR.9 until disbanding in May 1982.

In June 1982, following the disbandment of No. 39 Squadron, No. 1 Photographic Reconnaissance Unit formed at RAF Wyton with No. 39's PR.9s. The primary task of No. 1 PRU was maritime radar reconnaissance under the control of No. 18 (Maritime) Group, a task previously fulfilled by No. 27 Squadron, which operated four Vulcan B.2 (MRR) aircraft from RAF Scampton until its disbandment in April 1982.

The Canberra also had an important ELINT role to play. In August 1958, No. 192 Squadron at RAF Watton was renumbered No. 51 Squadron and was armed with four Canberra B.2s and four de Havilland Comet Mk 2Rs, the latter fitted out for electronic intelligence gathering. Also on the squadron's inventory was a Handley Page Hastings, for logistical support, and a Vickers Varsity; this was used to train signals specialists on flights along the East–West German border, these sorties being code-named *Baby Crawl*. The squadron operated throughout the NATO area, although the Canberras typically flew over the Baltic, monitoring Soviet transmissions on a 14-channel tape recorder mounted in the bomb bay. This equipment, of American design and also used in the RB-47, replaced an earlier, unsatisfactory wire recorder unit which was prone to breakages.

The usual technique employed was for the Canberra to transit to the operational area at high level (35,000 feet) in radio silence, obtaining radar fixes en route with the aid of Blue Shadow SLR. On approaching the operational area this would be switched off

Canberra PR.7 WH801 of No. 17 Squadron on a low-level photographic mission over Germany.

The Canberra T.17 was configured for ECM training.

Canberra T.17 WJ981 of No. 360 Squadron pictured at RAF Wyton.

and navigation carried out by Green Satin doppler. On entering the Baltic the aircraft would descend towards Swedish air space, as though to land in Sweden, coming down to 500 feet behind the island of Gotland, where it was effectively masked from Soviet radar. It would then fly north on its eavesdropping mission before turning east and then south, in international air space. The whole object was to capture and identify signals emanating from new equipment, and pinpoint the stations transmitting them, before the Russians were alerted to the presence of the aircraft. The Canberra would then climb back to 35,000 feet to make its exit from the Baltic.

The Comets, meanwhile, were engaged in much the same type of ferret activities as the USAF's RB-47s, monitoring signals traffic off northern Norway, over the Black Sea and the Middle East, with occasional deployments to the Far East. The northern flights were made from No. 51 Squadron's UK base, RAF Watton, the aircraft sometimes staging through Norwegian airfields; coverage of the Baltic would be made from Germany, while flights to the Black Sea were made from Cyprus. In addition to its flight crew (which included two navigators to ensure accuracy) each Comet carried ten specialist operators, including linguists to monitor Russian voice traffic. Much of the on-board electronic equipment was of American origin, and there was a good deal of co-operation between the Comet crews and their USAF counterparts in the 55th Strategic Reconnaissance Wing.

The last of the Comets was retired in 1974, at about the same time as the last of the squadron's Canberras; these were four B.Mk.6RCs (the RC standing for radar countermeasures). By then No. 51 Squadron had moved to RAF Wyton and had re-armed with Nimrod R.1 aircraft, which it still uses today.

Nimrod R.1 ELINT aircraft pictured at RAF Waddington, Lincolnshire. (Colin Lambert)

8

PR Canberras in the Middle East

THE FIRST RAF PR unit to convert to Canberras in the Middle East was No. 13 Squadron, which had hitherto operated Meteor PR.10s in the strategic reconnaissance role from Abu Sueir, Egypt, before moving to Akrotiri in Cyprus at the beginning of 1956. The squadron's first two Canberra PR.7s arrived in May 1956; these were WH775 (Flt Lt Adams and Fg Off Ramsay) and WH801 (Fg Off Campbell and Fg Off Toseland). By mid-September No. 13 Squadron had four PR.7s (WH799 and WT540, in addition to the pair mentioned earlier, as well as two T.4 trainers) but only two PR.7s were serviceable; the rest had various technical troubles – mostly fuel leaks – and WH801 had been damaged in a landing accident. Fortunately, most of these troubles had been sorted out by the last week in October, when the squadron was tasked with providing photographic coverage for Operation *Musketeer*, the Anglo-French Suez landings.

Prior to the Suez operations, No. 13 Squadron carried out trials with the F/Low Level/F95 camera, but these were handicapped by the 250-knot speed limitation imposed on the Canberra at low altitude, so the Canberra retained its high-level role while tactical low-level reconnaissance was carried out by French Air Force RF-84Fs, deployed to Cyprus. No. 13 Squadron also hosted a detachment of No. 58 Squadron, which had been operating from Akrotiri since 1 August 1956 in anticipation of the Suez action, and on 20 October – ten days before the outbreak of hostilities – a Canberra of this unit, with special Air Ministry authorisation, flew the first reconnaissance mission over Egyptian territory. The aircraft was PR.7 WJ921 (Flt Lt G. J. Clark), which surveyed the Egyptian coastline from 30,000 feet. A fighter escort was provided by French F-84Fs, but there was no reaction.

On 28 October No. 13 Squadron made its first operational sortie over Egypt, and had flown four more by the end of the month. On the second sortie, on 29 October, the Canberra crewed by Sqn Ldr Field and Fg Off Lever was the target of some ineffectual Egyptian anti-aircraft fire, and the next day PR.7 WT540, flown by Flt Lt Hunter (navigator Fg Off Urquhart-Pullen) was attacked by a MiG-15 and suffered slight cannon fire damage to the elevator. Also on 30 October, Fg Off Campbell and Fg Off Toseland had a narrow escape when explosive cannon shells were seen to pass on both sides of the cockpit. Evasive action threw off the attacker, which was not identified.

On 31 October, before the RAF implemented the first phase of *Musketeer* by bombing Egyptian airfields, the PR Canberras flew four more sorties over Egypt, gathering last-minute target data; the French RF-84Fs flew seven. In general, the

Oil storage tanks at Port Said, photographed by a Canberra from 47,000 feet.

A Canberra PR.7 of No. 13 Squadron, pictured at Akrotiri after being attacked by a MiG-15 and suffering cannon shell damage to its tail.

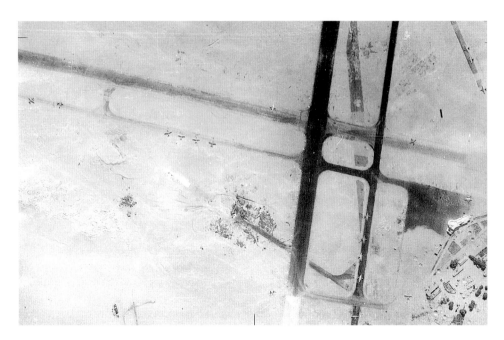

French PR organisation was much more efficient than the RAF's; the RF-84F unit (the *33eme Escadre*) had the necessary processing and interpretation facilities based alongside it and results were available very quickly, usually within an hour and a half. No. 13/58 Squadron's efforts, on the other hand, had to be sent into Episkopi for processing, which could result in a delay of up to seven hours before the photographs were to hand. Nevertheless, the overall PR coverage was excellent, and was to remain so throughout the campaign, although not all the results reached the right people, as Sqn Ldr Paul Mallorie – commanding No. 139 (Target Marker) Squadron – recalled:

> 'Intelligence was very sparse...when we came to study our targets what we had to look at were old pages torn out of pilots' handbooks from the time the British were there. We did not see, in the whole of the operation, a single current photograph of the airfields and defences that we were going against, although we did see photographs of our raid results afterwards.'

Sometimes, post-strike reconnaissance showed less than encouraging results. On the night of 1/2 November 1956, for example, main force Canberra crews returning from an attack on Luxor, where 20 Egyptian Ilyushin Il-28 jet bombers had been located, reported that the airfield had been badly hit, but a post-strike recce by a No. 13 Squadron Canberra at 12.40 GMT on 2 November told a different tale. No bombs had fallen on the airfield, and the Il-28s were still intact. It was left to a French F-84F strike from Israel to knock them out.

Concerns about an apparent build-up of Soviet-built combat aircraft in Syria resulted in part of No. 13/58 Squadron's effort being diverted in that direction. Allied Intelligence also knew of a plan, fostered by Egypt, called Operation *Beisan*, which envisaged an offensive by Syrian and Jordanian forces aimed at cutting Israel in two and reaching the Mediterranean at Nathanya. The PR operations over Syria resulted in

Opposite: *Ilyushin Il-28s at Luxor, photographed by a No. 13 Squadron Canberra on 2 November 1956.*

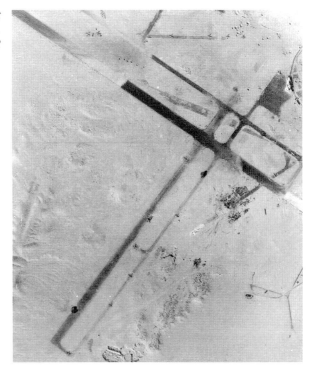

Luxor airfield, showing wrecked and burnt Il-28s after attacks by French F-84F Thunderstreaks operating from Israel.

Canberra PR.7 WH799 was shot down by a Syrian Meteor NF.13 while on a reconnaissance mission over Syria on 6 November 1956. One crew member was killed.

the RAF's only Canberra loss of the campaign, when PR.7 WH799 was intercepted by a Syrian Air Force Meteor NF.13 and shot down on 6 November. The navigator, Fg Off Urquhart-Pullen, was killed; the pilot, Flt Lt B. L. Hunter, and a third crew member were injured and detained in Beirut Military Hospital. They were later repatriated.

One of No. 13 Squadron's tasks after Suez, on behalf of AHQ Cyprus, was to undertake regular surveillance of airfields in Middle East countries which were being supplied with Soviet aircraft, and also to provide photographic coverage of new airfields. Several such clandestine flights were undertaken against unspecified airfield targets, (the tracks flown by the Canberras being referred to in the Squadron Operations Record Book as Routes, designated One, Two and so on) during 1957–8, No. 13 Squadron's aircraft being flown on occasions by No. 58 Squadron crews detached from the UK. Many of these flights had to be aborted due to contrails, which were sometimes in evidence up to 50,000 feet. If the urgency of the mission dictated that it had to be flown, whether contrails were present or not, the sortie was carefully planned so that the minimum time was spent in hostile air space.

In the summer of 1961, by which time Canberra PR.9s had replaced the PR.7s, a detachment of No. 13 Squadron was sent to Bahrain to provide pre-strike photographic coverage of airfield targets in Iraq at the time of the first Kuwait crisis, and remained there for some time even after the situation had been defused. In September 1962, the Squadron's PR.9s, together with aircraft of No. 58 Squadron deployed to Akrotiri from the UK, were sent to Khormaksar in order to photograph ports in the Yemen, where arms shipments were thought to be arriving from Egypt.

Surveillance of the Iraq–Kuwait frontier remained a Priority One task during 1963, and to meet this requirement a detachment of two Canberra PR.9s was maintained at RAF Muharraq on a more or less permanent basis. The Canberras flew a daily sortie at high altitude over the frontier and, in conditions of good visibility, were able to detect any unusual military movement well inside Iraq. The detachment was maintained by rotating crews once a week, which provided the opportunity for the aircraft to be flown back to Cyprus for second-line servicing. As the daily reconnaissance task did not utilise the full effort available from the two Canberras, the opportunity was taken to survey some of the more remote parts of Oman, which at that time was very inadequately mapped. The PR surveillance of the Iraqi frontier produced an alert towards the end of 1964, when the Canberras revealed concentrations of Iraqi armour close to the Kuwait border; an additional PR.9 was brought in from Akrotiri to strengthen the surveillance, but it turned out that the Iraqi Army was conducting manoeuvres. Nevertheless, a potential threat from Iraq persisted – and was underlined when, in 1967, Iraqi jets crossed the Kuwait border, allegedly by mistake – and so the PR surveillance continued.

In May 1970 No. 13 Squadron's Canberras were called in to make daily reconnaissance flights along the border between Abu Dhabi and Saudi Arabia, who

Almaza airfield, photographed from 30,000 feet by a Canberra of No. 13 Squadron on 1 November 1956. The aircraft on the ground are mostly Dakotas.

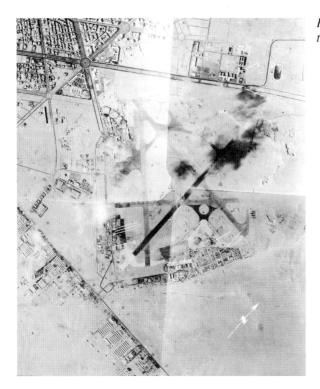

Photo-mosaic of Almaza after the initial Allied air strikes.

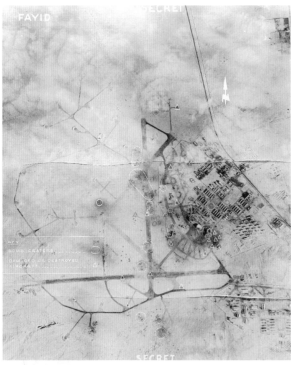

The airfield at Fayid seen after a heavy bombing attack.

Cairo West, with wrecked Ilyushin Il-28s in their blast pens.

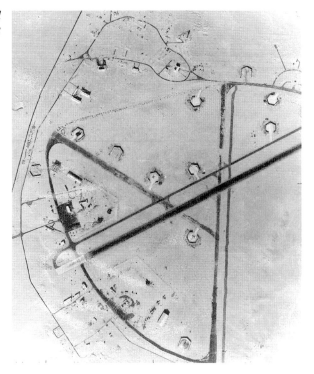

Cairo International Airport after a raid by RAF Valiants. Aircraft pictured include C-47s and a DC-6.

The remains of Nasser's C-47 transport fleet at Almaza after strikes by Fleet Air Arm aircraft.

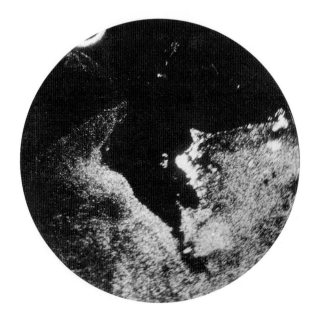

Radar photograph of the Egyptian coastline, taken by a Valiant.

were in dispute over oil drilling rights. The dispute was, however, settled by diplomatic means.

In 1971 British forces withdrew from their remaining bases in the Gulf area, resulting in a considerable reduction of No. 13 Squadron's PR task, and in October 1972 it moved from Cyprus to Luqa, Malta, to become the resident PR unit there. It was now NATO-assigned, and carried out designated tasks on behalf of the C-in-C Allied Forces Mediterranean until British forces withdrew from Malta in 1978, whereupon it returned to the United Kingdom in October to become established at RAF Wyton. Its PR.9s went to No. 39 Squadron, and it rearmed with PR.7s, having 14 aircraft on charge in 1980. It disbanded in the following year.

The unit which No. 13 Squadron had replaced in Malta was No. 39 Squadron, that had formed there in July 1958 with Canberra PR.3s re-allocated from the recently disbanded No. 69 Squadron in Germany. It was the only high-altitude PR squadron assigned to Allied Forces Southern Europe, and as such its operational area was very large, covering Greece, Italy, Turkey and the Mediterranean. In addition, it carried out photographic survey tasks over many parts of Africa and the Middle East. It began to receive Canberra PR.9s in October 1962, and with these took on the additional task of maritime reconnaissance, monitoring the growing Soviet naval presence in the Mediterranean. No. 39 Squadron returned to the United Kingdom in September 1970 and operated on NATO tasks out of RAF Wyton until May 1982, when it disbanded. Its PR.9s were turned over to the newly-formed No. 1 PRU.

9

Operations in the Western Pacific, 1953–65

BY THE END of the Korean War, the component squadrons of the 55th Strategic Reconnaissance Wing, which was the SAC unit primary responsible for ELINT missions, had re-equipped with the Boeing RB-50. At Yokota, the 55th SRW's Detachment Two, consisting of the 343rd SRS, used the RB-50G model, which was configured specifically for the ELINT role. (Other variants, the RB-50B and RB-50D, were configured for photo-mapping and photographic reconnaissance.)

Early in the morning of 29 July 1953, an RB-50G (serial number 47145) of the 343rd SRS took off from Yokota to carry out an ELINT mission in the Vladivostok area, a frequent target for such sorties. The aircraft carried six Ravens as well as its usual flight crew of eleven.

At about 06.15, the RB-50G was at 20,000 feet, some 26 miles off Cape Povorotny to the south-east of Vladivostok, when it was attacked by MiG-15s and two of its engines knocked out. The aircraft's starboard wing caught fire and began to disintegrate, collapsing and breaking away moments after the pilot, Captain Stanley O'Kelley, ordered the crew to bale out. Twenty hours later an American destroyer picked up Captain John E. Roche, the co-pilot and sole survivor of the 17-man crew. Roche stated that he had been accompanied in the water for a time by O'Kelley, but that the two men had lost contact and the pilot had presumably drowned.

Three bodies were later recovered after being washed ashore on the coast of Japan; 13 crewmen were listed as missing. In the years that followed, however, there were persistent reports that other crew members had also baled out and had been captured by the Russians; it was certain that Soviet patrol craft had combed the area – which was shrouded in mist at the time – because Roche had heard them. He also claimed to have heard the voices of fellow crew members, calling for help.

The USAF continued to insist that the aircraft (which it referred to as a B-50, not an RB-50) had been on a routine navigational training flight and that it had been shot down over international waters. The US State Department presented the Russians with a claim for $2,785,492.94, which included replacement of the aircraft and compensation for the families of the dead airmen. The Russians at once replied with a counter-claim for $1,861,450 in respect of a Russian Ilyushin Il-12 transport aircraft, shot down by an American F-86 Sabre on the last day of the war in Korea. The Il-12 had been flying from Lu-Shun in China to Vladivostok, taking a short cut across a narrow strip of North Korean territory that jutted into Manchuria, where lots of wreckage fell. All 21 on board – presumably Soviet military personnel who had been taking an active part in the war – were killed.

Was the shooting down of the RB-50 a reprisal for the destruction of the Il-12? That will never be known, but it seems certain that the Russians were lying in wait for the reconnaissance aircraft. The presence of Soviet naval craft at the exact place where the interception took place is evidence enough, and it seems likely that their crews had orders to rescue any surviving Americans and bring them ashore for interrogation. According to some sources, that is exactly what happened.

In 1991, with the Cold War over, the Russians and Americans agreed to establish a joint commission called Task Force Russia, its object being to investigate the fate of any Americans who might have fallen into Soviet hands after the end of the Second World War. The opening of this door enabled relatives of some missing airmen to visit Russia and make enquiries of their own; this included Bruce Sanderson, whose father, Lieutenant Warren J. Sanderson, was one of the RB-50 aircrew unaccounted for.

The North American AJ-1 Savage – the US Navy's first nuclear-capable bomber – was converted to the AJ-2P photo reconnaissance aircraft. The bomb bay could house up to seven cameras.

When Sanderson visited Moscow in the autumn of 1992 he met a former Soviet intelligence officer turned military historian called Gavril Korotkov, who was adamant that six airmen – including Lt Sanderson – were captured and interrogated by a KGB counter-espionage unit. Refusing to co-operate, the Americans were classed as spies and sent to Gadhala prison camp in south-central Siberia. If the story is true – and it is highly unlikely that it will ever be verified – it is improbable that any of the men would have survived their captivity.

The loss of the RB-50 led to future ELINT missions being provided with a fighter escort wherever possible, an arrangement that certainly saved an RB-50 on 22 January 1954 when it was attacked by MiGs over the Yellow Sea. The attackers were beaten off by 16 F-86F Sabres, which shot one of them down. Two more American reconnaissance aircraft, however, were lost in the northwestern Pacific in 1954. On 4 September, a P2V Neptune of Patrol Squadron VP-19 was attacked by two MiG-15s off the Siberian coast and forced to ditch in the Sea of Japan. On this occasion most of the crew were lucky; although one went down with the aircraft, nine were rescued. But only three days later, an RB-29 was shot down into the Sea of Japan off Hokkaido with the loss of 13 crew.

The toll was mounting, and not only reconnaissance aircraft were the victims. On 23 July 1954, a Cathay Pacific airliner was shot down by Chinese fighters off Hainan Island, and three days later two AD Skyraiders of Air Group 5 from the carrier USS *Philippine Sea*, searching for survivors, were attacked by a pair of La-7s or La-9s. The US Navy pilots turned the tables and destroyed both Chinese aircraft.

On 17 April 1955 the Russian fighters scored their first success against the new Boeing RB-47E Stratojet when a 55th SRW aircraft, on detachment to Japan, was shot down off Kamchatka, possibly by MiG-17s. Since 1954 the *Fresco*, to give the MiG-17 its NATO code-name, had been replacing the MiG-15 in the Soviet Air Force's far eastern fighter regiments, and its presence – as was the case in the west – stripped the RB-47 of the relative immunity it had enjoyed so far.

In June 1955 a new type of aircraft joined the electronic war in the northwestern Pacific when Electronic Countermeasures Squadron VQ-1, the first of its kind in the US Navy, was commissioned at Iwakuni, Japan, with Martin P4M-1Q Mercators. The Mercator had been in service with Patrol Squadron VP-21 since 1950, and the power of its twin Pratt & Whitney Wasp Major radial engines was augmented by two Allison J33 turbojets. VQ-1 began operations almost immediately, flying ELINT missions along the Chinese and Siberian coasts.

On 22 July 1955 the US Navy lost another Neptune, when a P2V-5 of VP-9 on a mission off the western Aleutians was attacked by two MiG-15s. With its starboard engine in flames the Neptune crash-landed on St Lawrence Island, in Alaskan territory south of the Bering Strait. Although there were injuries among the crew, there were no fatalities.

The late 1950s saw a period of high tension between the Republic of China (Nationalist China) Government on the island of Taiwan and the communist Chinese People's Republic, the principal flashpoints being the nationalist-occupied offshore islands of Quemoy and Matsu, to which the communists laid claim, and much of the US Navy's surveillance activities were concentrated on this disputed area. On 22 August 1956, a P4M Mercator of VQ-1 out of Iwakuni, on night patrol 32 miles off the Chinese mainland, reported that it was under attack by fighters over international waters and was not heard from again. Carrier and land-based aircraft and surface vessels, searching the area, found wreckage, empty life rafts and the bodies of two

In the early 1950s the US Navy produced photo-recce variants of its two principal jet fighters, the McDonnell F2H Banshee and the Grumman F9F Panther.

The Lockheed Neptune was the US Navy's principal long-range reconnaissance aircraft during the 1950s and early 1960s.

crew members. Only weeks later, on 10 September, an RB-50 on a photo-mapping sortie was shot down over the Sea of Japan.

On 16 June 1959 another P4M Mercator of VQ-1, operating off the west coast of Korea, was attacked by two MiG-17s. Their gunfire wounded one crewman and put both starboard engines (piston and turbojet) out of action, as well as damaging some of the flight controls. Despite this, the pilot made a successful emergency landing at Miho, Japan.

By the middle of 1959 the principal China ELINT and photographic surveillance tasks had been taken over by RB-57s and RF-101 Voodoos, and the last of VQ-1's Mercators was retired in May the following year. There were no further attacks on American aircraft for some time, either off the Chinese coast or off Siberia, but interceptions were frequent, as an extract from the operations summary of Patrol Squadron VP-22 shows. This unit, equipped with Neptunes, was on WESTPAC (Western Pacific) deployment during most of 1962, flying reconnaissance and anti-submarine patrols over the Sea of Japan, and in the Tsugaru and Soya Straits, the former between the Japanese islands of Honshu and Hokkaido and the latter between Hokkaido and the southern tip of Sakhalin. VP-22 crews logged the following encounters with Soviet aircraft:

(Author's note. Some of the abbreviations used in the summary have been transposed into plain language for ease of reading.)

3 May 1962. Time 0458Z (GMT). Position 43.24N 136.40E. Two Russian *Frescos* (MiG-17s) intercepted QA-3 which was heading 045 at 180 kts. The *Frescos* initially passed abeam to port, heading 235°T, then orbited aft of the P2V and passed again abeam to port. The *Frescos* then crossed the bow and ascended from 1,500 to 2,500 ft. During all the passes, abeam, forward and aft, distance was approx. 1,000 yards.

From 1962, the Neptune was progressively replaced by the Lockheed P-3 Orion, a maritime version of the Electra airliner.

During the intercept, QA-3 maintained 1,500 ft, course 045, speed 180 knots. The total time held was eleven minutes.

6 May 1962. Time 0258Z. Position 42.32N 135.40E. Two Russian *Frescos* intercepted QA-8 while rigging (identifying and photographing) the Russian freighter *Uman*. The P2V was at 200 ft, course/speed 051/160 kts. The *Frescos* passed 100 yards abeam to starboard at 250 ft, then crossed the bow at 1,500 yards, then abeam to port approx. 14,000 yards climbing to 2,500 ft. During the intercept, QA-8 ascended to 1,500 ft and altered heading to 071°T. The total time held was ten minutes.

8 May 1962. Time 0225Z. Position 44.27N 138.10E. Two Russian *Frescos* (side numbers 31 and 51) intercepted QA-2. QA-2 was tracking a Russian freighter. The *Frescos* were in a loose tail chase formation approx eight miles apart. No. 31 passed 100 yards to starboard at 200 ft above the P2V, then orbited 2,500 yards to starboard then to port. No. 51 passed abeam to port at approx. one mile. During the intercept, QA-3 completed the rig and proceeded on track. The total time held was eight minutes.

11 May 1962. Time 0254Z. Position 42.29N 135.28E. Two Russian *Frescos* intercepted QA-6 which was heading 226°T at 170 kts. The altitude was 1,500 ft. Initially one *Fresco* paralleled QA-6 at 1,500 yards and made slow 'S' turns to maintain his position. After 25 minutes, as the first *Fresco* was breaking off in an ascending turn, the second passed to port and joined the other *Fresco*. During the intercept, the P2V maintained course/speed and altitude. Closest approach was 1,500 yards. Total time held was 27 minutes.

30 May 1962. Time 0414Z. Position 42.06N 134.48E. A Russian *Madge* (Beriev Be-6

long-range reconnaissance flying boat) was sighted on heading 080°T at 150 kts, 3,000 ft altitude. The P2V remained on heading 237°T at 1,500 ft throughout the sighting. Closest approach was 5,000 yards. Total time of sighting was two and a half minutes.

31 May 1962. Time 0018Z. Position 42.40N 135.35E. Two Russian *Frescos* intercepted QA-9, making three orbits closing to 1,500 yards and departed. P2V maintained course/speed and altitude throughout. Closest approach 1,500 yards. Total time held was ten minutes.

2 June 1962. Time 0153Z. Position 42.24N 135.35E. Two Russian *Frescos* intercepted P2V; made two wide orbits. P2V maintained course 055°T until 0205Z then altered heading to 040°T to conform to track. P2V maintained altitude of 2,000 ft throughout. Russian GCI heard on 130.0 m/c. P2V experienced radar interference during interceptors' approach. Interference consisted of 20 degree die-shaped sector with dashed lines around radiating to interceptors. Closest approach 2,000 yards. Total time held was 34 minutes.

7 June 1962. Time 0041Z. Position 42.31N 135.44E. Russian *Fresco* intercepted QA-5. The *Fresco* remained at about 500 ft and orbited overhead. The P2V was at 1,000 ft and maintained course and speed. Closest approach one nm. Total time held was six minutes.

9 June 1962. Time 0228Z. Position 41.53N 135.23E. Two unknown aircraft paced QA-10 for 1 hour and 47 minutes. ECM and radar both held the aircraft intermittently. One visual sighting was made; a reflection from the sun was observed from the area of the contacts. Closest approach 18 nm.

10 June 1962. Time 0022Z. Position 45.20N 138.55E. Two Russian *Frescos* Nos 08 and 61 intercpted QA-1. No. 61 passed approx. 25 ft abeam to starboard, waved, caused the P2V to get into the jet slipstream, made two slow rolls and departed. During the intercept, the P2V attempted to alter heading from approx. 065°T to 090°T and had to hold it because one of the *Frescos* rode abeam to starboard. Total time held was eight minutes.

13 June 1962. Time 0128Z. Position 41.44N 133.48E. One probable Russian *Madge* was sighted course/speed 250°T/150 kts at 1,500 ft. P2V continued on course of 070°T. Closest approach eight nm.
- 0154Z, 41.57N 135.30E: QA-2 intercepted one Russian *Madge* No. 09. The P2V was heading 045°T at 1,500 ft; the *Madge* was on course 240°T. The *Madge* altered heading to 060°T and the P2V passed aft and then altered heading to 060°T to parallel the *Madge* at which time (0157Z) a Russian *Fresco* was sighted for approx. ten seconds at 42.03N 135.06E descending at approx. 45° from 3,000 ft, range 3 nm. The P2V continued on 060 and passed 500 ft abeam to port of the *Madge*. Closest approach three nm. The total time held was 15 minutes.

17 June 1962. Time 0213Z. Position 42.56N 136.13E. Two Russian *Frescos* made three 'S' turns 1,000 yards behind P2V QA-9, slowing down and losing altitude on starboard side. At approx. 2,000 ft the *Frescos* started typical flat side run across P2V tail and passed on port side. Course 219, speed 220 kts. Altitude 2,400 ft. Closest approach 1,000 yards. P2V straight and level. Time held four minutes.

19 June 1962. Time 0213Z. Position 42.16N 135.24E. Two Russian *Frescos* crossed back and forth behind US aircraft (QA-10) and made approx. five crossings and two level gunnery runs. Course 120 speed 300 kts. Altitude 700 to 3,000 ft. P2V making rig run during intercept. Closest approach 200 ft. Total time held five minutes.

25 June 1962. Time 0240Z. Position 42.37N 137.49E. Two Russian *Frescos* side numbers 04 and 11. *Frescos* straddled P2V (QA-2) then orbited. Tail chase formation. Course 230 speed 165 kts. Altitude 1,500 ft. P2V straight and level. Closest approach 100 yards. Total time held 20 minutes.

3 July 1962. Time 0156Z. Position 44.45N 137.49E. Two Russian *Frescos* side numbers 14 and 33. *Frescos* crossed from port to starboard and starboard to port, over and under, behind and in front of P2V, approx. 15 runs. Course 057 speed 200 kts. Altitude 1,500 ft. P2V straight and level. Closest approach 50 ft. Total time held was 14 minutes.

7 July 1962. Time 0209Z. Position 44.43N 137.50E. Two Russian *Frescos* side numbers 07 and 11 made ten overhead passes from rear, starboard and port side. Course 050 speed 150 kts. Altitude 1,000 ft. P2V (QA-9) straight and level. Closest approach 50 ft. Total time held was 13 minutes.

3 August 1962. Time 0141Z. Position 42.28N 135.08E. Two Russian *Frescos* made loose tail chase and passed on port side parallel to P2V (QA-3). Course 290 speed 200 kts. Altitude 1,500 ft. P2V straight and level. Closest approach one mile. Total time held was two minutes.

9 August 1962. Time 0448Z. Position 41.36N 134.26E. One probable Russian *Fresco* made one high speed overhead run. Course 205 speed 250 kts. Altitude 2,000 ft. P2V (QA-1) straight and level. Closest approach 200 yards. Total time held 30 seconds.

12 September 1962. Time 0352Z. Position 45.09N 139.25E. Two Russian *Frescos*, one side number 51. One *Fresco* remained high and aft at 3,000 ft. Other *Fresco* off starboard wing. Course 050 speed 200 kts. Altitude 500 ft. P2V (QA-1) straight and level. Closest approach 50 yards. Total time held was three minutes.

13 September 1962. Time 0644Z. Position 40.57N 131.25E. One Russian *Madge*, side number 14. P2V (QA-9) intercepted *Madge* and made one level pass off port wing. Course 010 speed 175 kts. Altitude 1,800 ft. Closest approach 500 ft. Total time held was six minutes.

14 September 1962. Time 0557Z. Position 45.00N 138.43E. Two Russian *Frescos* side numbers 38 and 62 made seven passes from aft. Course 175 speed 200 kts. Altitude from 500 to 200 ft. P2V (QA-2) descended to rig ship. Closest approach 30 ft. Total time held was 17 minutes.

22 September 1962. Time 0725Z. Position 45.46N 139.50E. Two *Frescos* side numbers 01 and 02. Six runs above and below P2V (QA-5). Orbiting speed 200 knots. Altitude 300 ft P2V straight and level. Closest approach 50 ft. Total time held was 20 minutes.

23 September 1962. Time 0316Z. Position 45.46N 139.07E. Two Russian *Frescos* side numbers 15 and 64 made two diving runs. Course 090 speed 200 kts. Altitude 5,000 ft. P2V (QA-2) straight and level at 3,000 ft. Closest approach 100 ft. Total time held was four minutes.

Such an intercept log was fairly typical for a USN maritime patrol squadron operating in the Sea of Japan area, with its sensitive and heavily defended Soviet naval installations. But VP-22's task was to increase, and the potential dangers multiply, during the last weeks of its tour of duty in Japan, for in October 1962 the Cuban Missile Crisis developed. The relevant part of VP-22's report, then classified 'Secret', reads:

'From 1 October 1962 to 19 November 1962, the 'Chop' date of the squadron's WESTPAC deployment, Patrol Squadron TWENTY-TWO was busily engaged in flying its reconnaissance patrols in the Sea of Japan, and in the Soya and Tsuragu Straits. This period highlighted the entire WESTPAC deployment, as the squadron actively participated in operations such as Victor-50, the Soviet Northern Sea Route Convoy, and many other demanding operations such as those performed under Defense Condition THREE set in the Pacific Fleet in October 1962. During these remaining few weeks in Japan, the squadron flew approximately 1,324 hours, 695 hours of which were flown in Tactical Antisubmarine Warfare flights required by DEFCON THREE. In these same few weeks VP-22 rigged over 320 surface vessels, fifty-five of which were Russian naval vessels, including ten Russian submarines. In addition, two other possible submarine contacts were developed, but not positively identified due to their proximity to the Russian coast. Several photographs were obtained of the six Russian FRESCO and FLASHLIGHT (Yakovlev Yak-25 all-weather interceptor – Author) type aircraft that were encountered, and others were sighted at a greater distance, almost daily, during the tense situation caused by the Cuban crisis. ECM and NAVCM collection gathering efforts played an important role during the entire deployment, and the intelligence gathered in this aspect resulted in many verbal communications being received from higher commands. Of primary concern during the deployment was the photography and Ear Trumpet (code name for a project dealing with obtaining multi-channel recordings of Russian submarines' underwater sounds), information which was received on merchant, naval and especially Russian submarine contacts. In this field the squadron also enjoyed high success.'

The Cuban crisis was resolved and there was an easing in the worldwide tension it had generated, but US reconnaissance operations off the sensitive communist coastlines of the north-west Pacific sometimes attracted bursts of gunfire from intercepting fighters, especially when surveillance of China was stepped up in October 1964 after the Chinese detonated their first nuclear device. On 27 April 1965 an RB-47H of the 55th SRW in an ELINT mission off the Korean coast was attacked by two North Korean MiG-17s. The RB-47 crew managed to beat off their attackers after a furious defensive battle in which they used the Stratojet's twin 20 mm tail cannon to good effect, but the aircraft sustained severe damage, two engines being knocked out and several systems being rendered inoperative. The two pilots, Lt Col Hobert D. Mattisen and 1st Lt Henry E. Dubury, made a skilful emergency landing at Yokota air base in Japan, but the RB-47 was a write-off.

10

America's Reconnaissance Canberra: The RB-57

IN THE IMMEDIATE post-war years, one of the key figures – perhaps *the* key figure – in promoting the necessity for high-altitude strategic reconnaissance was Colonel Richard S. Leghorn. As chief of the Eighth Air Force's 67th Reconnaissance Group in Europe during the Second World War he had overseen all pre-D-Day and post-D-Day reconnaissance during the period of the Normandy landings, and who in 1946 had been appointed Deputy Commander of Task Unit 1.52, which was responsible for photographing the results of the US atomic weapons tests at Bikini Atoll.

Leghorn's experiences during the war had convinced him that it would be possible to keep track of threatening developments by high-altitude photographic surveillance of potential enemies; he saw this as the only sure way of preventing surprise attacks such as the December 1941 Japanese raid on Pearl Harbor.

During the next few years Leghorn worked hard to persuade the authorities that the development and deployment of a new high-altitude strategic reconnaissance aircraft, equipped with high-resolution cameras, was of great importance. Late in 1950, he was appointed to head a reconnaissance division at Wright-Patterson AFB, and when he reported for duty in April 1951 his first action was to make a survey of the western world's aircraft manufacturers to discover which made the highest-flying aircraft. He felt strongly that any aircraft capable of exceeding 60,000 feet stood a good chance of evading Soviet fighters in the foreseeable future, as high-altitude SAMs would not be a threat for some years to come.

Leghorn soon established that the aircraft best suited to the high-altitude reconnaissance role at that time was the English Electric Canberra, which was just entering service in its B.2 light bomber version with RAF Bomber Command and which had been selected (in March 1951) for the USAF as a B-26 replacement. It was to be licence-built by the Glenn L. Martin Aircraft Company of Baltimore, Maryland, as the B-57. In the late summer of 1951, at Leghorn's request, English Electric sent a team of engineers and designers to Wright-Patterson to investigate the possibility of turning the Canberra into a very high altitude reconnaissance aircraft by reconfiguring it with very long, high-lift wings, two new Rolls-Royce Avon 109 engines, a single pilot rather than a crew of three, and an airframe that was stressed to less than the USAF's requirements. It was thought that such an aircraft might reach 63,000 feet

The Martin B-57A, the licence-built version of the Canberra B.2.

before penetrating hostile territory and, as its fuel supply diminished, might eventually climb to 67,000 feet. Leghorn's unit subsequently produced a study paper recommending a proposal for an aircraft that could penetrate hostile territory to a radius of 700 nautical miles. Deployed around the periphery of the Soviet Union and the People's Republic of China, such an aircraft could photograph up to 85 per cent of the targets in the two countries.

In the meantime, the USAF acquired its first reconnaissance Canberra variant, the tactical RB-57A, more or less by accident. After the selection of the Canberra to equip several squadrons of the USAF Tactical Air Command, it had been decided to implement a list of recommended design changes. While this list was being drawn up, production of the B-57A went ahead and the first aircraft was rolled out on 20 July 1953. The aircraft was externally similar to the Canberra B.2 except that the navigator's window was positioned aft of the cockpit on the starboard side, the windows on the port side of the fuselage being deleted. At this point, Martin received instructions to proceed with production of the revised B-57 design under the designation B-57B. Only eight aircraft were built to the B-57A bomber configuration; the next 67 were produced for the tactical reconnaissance role as RB-57As.

The first unit to equip with the RB-57A, late in 1954, was the 363rd Tactical Reconnaissance Wing at Shaw Air Force Base, South Carolina, but the principal users were the 10th and 66th TRWs (USAFE), based respectively at Spangdahlem in Germany and Laon in France. A number of these aircraft retained their natural metal finish, but most were covered in a special anti-searchlight matt black paint which, used on P-61 Black Widow night-fighters during the Second World War, made them virtually invisible in a searchlight beam.

The crews of the 10th and 66th TRW were generally pleased with the RB-57A, which was a long way in advance of the RB-26Cs with which they had previously been armed, although in its early service the aircraft was troubled by a series of mysterious crashes which also affected the RAF's Canberra B.2s. The cause was identified as a runaway tailplane trim actuator, but this was not established until the aircraft had been operational for some time. Nevertheless, crews were impressed with the RB-57A's manoeuvrability, which endowed it with a high survival factor in simulated combat with the jet fighters current at the time, and with its stability at all altitudes.

The 10th and 66th TRWs were assigned to the 4th Allied Tactical Air Force, on NATO's Central Front. In addition to their primary role of night photographic reconnaissance they also had a target marking role. Operationally, they were hampered by their high accident rate, which caused the RB-57As to be grounded during much of 1955. Beginning in April 1957 the 10th TRW began to rearm with the Douglas RB-66D, the last of these aircraft being delivered in December that year, but it was not until November 1958 that the final RB-57A was relinquished. In 1958 the 66th TRW also re-equipped too, with the McDonnell RF-101A Voodoo. The RB-57As were transferred to four Air National Guard squadrons, which retained them until the 1970s.

On 27 March 1953, as part of a highly classified programme known as *Black Knight*, the US Defense Department had issued a requirement (Design Study Requirement No. 53WC-16507) calling for a single-seat subsonic high-altitude reconnaissance aircraft capable of carrying a 700 lb payload over 3,000 miles at 70,000 feet. Three companies responded to the Air Force requirement.

Martin proposed the modified version of the B-57 Canberra, while Bell Aircraft and the Fairchild Aircraft Company each submitted entirely new designs. The Martin proposal was accepted, although it was considered as an interim aircraft while work proceeded on a better design.

Martin's design was the Model 294 B-57D (later changed to RB-57D) which had a standard B-57B fuselage married to a new wing with a span increased from 64 to 108 feet. The aircraft was powered by uprated J57-P-9 turbojets, was a single-seater and was equipped with two K-38 and two KC-1 split vertical cameras.

The EB-57E was used to evaluate electronic warfare systems. The last examples were withdrawn in 1982.

Six Model 294 RB-57Ds were ordered, followed by seven Model 744 RB-57Ds which were similar to the earlier model but had a flight refuelling capability. The next six aircraft, designated RB-57D-2 (Company designation Model 796) carried a crew of two; like the previous batch they had a flight refuelling capability but had a specialist ELINT/SIGINT role. The final variant, the RB-57D-1, was a single-seater fitted out for radar mapping day and night, being equipped with the AN/APQ-56 SLR. Only one aircraft was delivered.

Despite stressing problems with the new big wing, the RB-57D was accepted for service by the USAF and the first examples were delivered to the 4025th Strategic Reconnaissance Squadron of the 4080th SRW in March 1956. Following operational training, detachments were sent to Yokota in Japan and Eielson AFB, Alaska. The Alaskan detachment carried out ELINT operations around the Kamchatka peninsula for a short period before returning to its home base at Ramey AFB, Puerto Rico. The Japanese detachment, on the other hand, remained at Yokota from October 1956 to September 1957 on a task code-named Operation *Sea Lion*, monitoring radiation samples from Soviet nuclear tests and gathering electronic intelligence on Soviet naval and air force operations in the Far East. Some sorties were also flown over Communist China. The RB-57D operated at altitudes of up to 55,000 feet, so its operations were restricted to intelligence targets around the periphery of hostile territory in the case of the USSR; monitoring Chinese targets presented less of a problem, for the RB-57D's ceiling was outside the scope of the CPAF's MiG-15s.

The 4025th SRS also sent an RB-57D detachment of four aircraft to Rhein-Main air base in Germany (Operation *Bordertown*) to carry out ELINT/SIGINT missions along the German border and over the Baltic. RB-57s returning from sorties over the Baltic were often intercepted by RAF Hawker Hunter fighters of 2 ATAF, scrambled to make an identification check of the inbound aircraft, as the lone reconnaissance missions were flown in complete secrecy. When the 4025th SRS was deactivated in June 1959 the four RB-57s at Rhein-Main were assigned to a new unit, the 7407th Support Squadron, which came under the orders of HQ USAFE. The 7407th SS's strength was raised to six aircraft with the addition of two more RB-57Ds, including the sole RB-57D-1 with its high-resolution AN/APQ-56 SLR. These aircraft continued to fly intelligence-gathering missions on behalf of USAFE until 1964, when increasing structural fatigue problems with the wing caused the RB-57D to be withdrawn from service.

After the 4025th SRS was deactivated in 1959, some of its RB-57Ds were adapted to other specialist tasks. Some were used by NASA for high-altitude tests and terrain mapping, while four were assigned to the 4677th Radar Evaluation Squadron for calibration duties. Six more RB-57Ds were used to monitor the last series of American atmospheric nuclear tests in 1962, taking radiation samples in the upper atmosphere. Three RB-57Ds were operated by the 1211th Test Squadron (Sampling) of the US Air Weather Service at Kirtland AFB, New Mexico, and were re-designated WB-57Ds; this unit later became the 58th Weather Reconnaissance Squadron.

In 1966, two years after its wing structural problems had led to the RB-57D's retirement, Martin received a USAF contract to rebuild the wings of eight stored aircraft with a guaranteed 3,000-hour fatigue life. These aircraft were fitted with a range of ECM equipment and were used in the defence evaluation role until 1970, when they were once again placed in storage. In this final role the aircraft were designated EB-57D.

In 1958, at a time when the Chinese communists were shelling the offshore islands of Quemoy and Matsu and threatening an invasion of Taiwan itself, the US Central Intelligence Agency initiated a project code-named *Diamond Lil*, which led to a programme of overflights of the Chinese mainland by RB-57D aircraft flown by Chinese Nationalist Air Force aircrew. Six CNAF pilots were trained on the B-57C at Laughlin AFB, Texas; they returned to Taiwan in January 1959 and three RB-57Ds were ferried to Taoyuan air base, near Taipei, by US pilots. Two B-57Cs were also deployed to Taoyuan from the USAF 3rd Bomb Wing's base at Yokota for continuation training. During the early part of 1959 the three RB-57s carried out many surveillance flights over mainland China, photographing CPAF airfields and military establishments, while ports that might have been used for the assembly of an invasion force were photographed by RF-101C Voodoos, also flown by CNAF pilots. One RB-57D was lost when it apparently suffered pressurisation failure at altitude and had to make an emergency descent over the Chinese coast, where it was shot down by MiGs. The other two RB-57Ds continued to operate until 1964, when fatigue problems with the wing main spar forced their withdrawal.

In 1962, with main spar fatigue troubles already grounding a sizeable part of the RB-57D fleet, the USAF approached General Dynamics – who had a contract for maintaining and updating the RB-57D – to see if it would be feasible to revamp the existing B-57 design and produce what would be virtually a new reconnaissance aircraft with enhanced all-round performance, improved payload capacity and extended fatigue life. Studies proceeded under the direction of Vincent Dolson, the head of special projects at General Dynamics' Fort Worth Division, and in October 1962 authority was given for the construction of two redesigned aircraft under the designation RB-57F. The project was given high priority and the first RB-57F was rolled out on 16 May 1963, making its first flight on 23 June.

The aircraft that emerged from Forth Worth bore only a superficial resemblance to the Canberra that was its progenitor. It was almost completely redesigned and rebuilt, and General Dynamics made extensive use of new materials, including honeycomb sandwich panels, for the new components. Much of this technology had been developed for the Convair/GD B-58 Hustler supersonic bomber. The RB-57F's wing was an entirely new, three-spar structure with the enormous span of 122 feet 5 inches and a marked anhedral. The ailerons were inset at mid-span and were supplemented by spoilers. All control surfaces had tightly-sealed gaps to reduce drag, and there were no flaps. To improve longitudinal and asymmetric control at altitude the aircraft was fitted with larger vertical tail surfaces with twice the area of the standard B-57's.

The 7,220 lbst Wright J-65 turbojets used in earlier marks of B-57 were replaced by two 18,000 lbst Pratt & Whitney TF33-P-11A turbofan engines, giving the RB-57F more than double the power of its predecessors. Provision was also made for a 3,300 lbst Pratt & Whitney J60-P-9 turbojet in a detachable pod under each wing. These were air-started, remaining at idling rpm up to 32,000 feet, when partial throttle control became effective. Full throttle could be used above 42,000 feet. The RB-57F had four underwing hard points, all of which could be used to carry external stores when the turbojets were not mounted.

The fuselage tanks were deleted to make room for special equipment, all fuel being carried in the wings outboard of the engines. The bulkiest system carried by the aircraft was the two-ton HTAC high-altitude camera, which was capable of taking high-resolution photographs of targets at an oblique range of up to 60 miles from high altitude. Other special ELINT/SIGINT equipment was carried in the redesigned nose and in the plastic wingtip sections. The cockpit layout was unchanged, with ejection seats in tandem for the crew of two, and was fitted with a modified Lear MC-1 autopilot of the type used in the Boeing C-135 transport aircraft.

Late in 1963 the first two RB-57Fs were sent for operational trials with the 7407th Combat Support Wing at Rhein-Main air base, from where they made a series of high-altitude reconnaissance flights at altitudes of up to 60,000 feet along the East German border and over the Baltic. In February 1964, following these trials, they were assigned to the 58th Weather Reconnaissance Squadron at Kirtland AFB, New Mexico.

The USAF awarded a contract to General Dynamics for the construction of 19 more RB-57Fs, most of which were assigned to the 9th Weather Reconnaissance Wing at McLelland AFB, California. The RB-57Fs were divided between four of the 9th WRW's squadrons, the 55th, 56th, 57th and 58th. One of these, the 55th, remained at MacLelland AFB, the 56th was deployed to Yokota air base in Japan, the 57th operated out of RAAF Avalon, Australia, and the 58th remained at Kirtland. All these RB-57Fs were used in the primary meteorological role, carrying out atmospheric sampling and radiation detection, but they also had a secondary reconnaissance role and could be called upon to make overflights of potential trouble spots.

Four of the 19 RB-57Fs operated purely as reconnaissance aircraft, two being deployed to Yokota and the other pair to Rhein-Main with the 7407th Combat Support Squadron. On 14 December 1965, one of the aircraft with the latter unit was shot down

One of three RB-57Fs used by NASA on research work in connection with the US space programme.

over the Black Sea by a Soviet SAM while carrying out a close-range surveillance mission off Odessa. Part of the wreckage was recovered by a US naval task force, but no trace of the crew was ever found.

In 1968 the Air Weather Service's RB-57Fs were redesignated WB-57F and continued to be used in the atmospheric sampling role, mostly on behalf of the Atomic Energy Commission. Some were fitted with probes mounted on the nose or engine nacelles, which picked up particles after a nuclear explosion and enabled scientists to determine their path and intensity. Much of this activity was centred on nuclear tests in China and India, but the WB-57Fs were also used to monitor US air space in the aftermath of underground tests. At least one WB-57F was used in connection with research into early airborne laser equipment, and three were used by NASA in connection with the US space programme. The USAF gradually phased out its remaining WB-57Fs during the 1970s and placed them in storage at Davis-Monthan AFB, but NASA continued to use its aircraft on research work until the early 1980s.

Two USAF RB-57Fs were loaned to Pakistan shortly before that country's 1965 war with India, but one of these was returned to the USA shortly before the outbreak of hostilities and stayed there. The original reason for the deployment of the RB-57Fs to Pakistan was that it provided a convenient base from which to monitor Chinese nuclear testing, which began with the explosion of a device in October 1964, and the aircraft were flown by USAF crews during these operations. The RB-57F that remained in Pakistan was operated, with US agreement, by No. 24 Squadron Pakistan Air Force, and was based at Mauripur near Karachi. During the war it operated alongside two RB-57Bs, jamming Indian R/T transmissions and monitoring the daily position of the Indian Army's mobile radar units. As much of the equipment used by the Indians was of Soviet manufacture, these sorties provided useful information for American analysts.

The RB-57F made daily sorties over principal Indian Air Force airfields at altitudes of up to 65,000 feet, well above the ceiling of IAF fighters, but on 15 September 1965 it was straddled by two SA2 *Guideline* SAMs at 52,000 feet as it was beginning its letdown towards Peshawar from Ambala. One SAM exploded just above the aircraft and another below it, causing major structural damage and knocking out both auxiliary turbojets. Despite this, and the fact that its nosewheel would not extend, the pilot nursed the aircraft to Peshawar and made a successful forced landing. More than 170 holes, the biggest more than a foot in diameter, were found in the aircraft. It was repaired by Pakistan Air Force technicians and later returned to the USA.

11

Black Angel: The Lockheed U-2

CURIOUSLY ENOUGH, ALTHOUGH it had a wealth of experience in high-altitude photographic reconnaissance and jet aircraft design – it had been responsible for the PR version of the P-38 Lightning and the P-80, America's first operational jet fighter – the Lockheed Aircraft Corporation of Burbank, California, had not been issued with the USAF requirement that resulted in the high-level Canberra, the Martin B-57D. However, the Lockheed design team under the direction of Clarence 'Kelly' Johnson, the Corporation's Chief Engineer, proceeded with design studies of its own, and in March 1954 Johnson presented his proposal to the Air Force. Known as the Lockheed Model CL-282, the design was based on the fuselage and tail unit of a Lockheed F-104 Starfighter mated with a very high aspect ratio wing. At that time the Starfighter was the fastest, highest flying fighter in the world, having reached a speed of over 1,400 mph and an altitude of 103,395 feet.

The proposal was rejected on the grounds of the chosen engine; Johnson wanted the experimental General Electric J73, while the USAF favoured the proven Pratt & Whitney J57. The Air Force's caution was understandable; with long flights over hostile territory envisaged, engine reliability meant survival.

Meanwhile, the US military hierarchy and the various intelligence agencies had been working hard to persuade the new US President, Dwight D. Eisenhower, that overflights of the Soviet Union could be undertaken without seriously jeopardizing US–Soviet relations or, at worst, starting a war. One of the key arguments used was that the aircraft performing the mission would be virtually undetectable, and on 24 November 1954 Eisenhower was persuaded by two very influential and well-trusted advisers, James Killian and Edwin Land, that an aircraft could overfly the USSR without being detected. They did not pretend that it would be invisible; simply that it would evade detection. The theory was that if it could reach an altitude significantly greater than 40,000 feet while still outside the 200-mile range of the Russians' SCR-270 early warning radar, the SCR-585 anti-aircraft, automatic tracking radars would not be alerted to the presence of an intruder and would not be activated. At this time, Killian was chairman and Land a member of the Technological Capabilities Panel, empowered by Eisenhower to advise him on the Soviet threat; he accepted their recommendations, although with some reservations that an aircraft flying straight and level for long distances over hostile territory might still be vulnerable to interception.

Also in November 1954, Kelly Johnson, undeterred by the Air Force's rejection of his proposal, submitted it to officials of the Central Intelligence Agency, and following a meeting with CIA Director Allan Dulles and the agency's Chief of Research and Development, Dr Joe Charyk, agreement was reached whereby Johnson would redesign the CL-282 around the Pratt & Whitney J57 turbojet, while still incorporating many of the F-104's features. Johnson indicated that Lockheed could build 20 aircraft plus spares for $22 million, and that a prototype would be ready within eight months of signing a contract.

On 9 December 1954 the CIA awarded Lockheed a development contract under the code name Project *Aquatone*, with funds for the airframes to be provided by the CIA and USAF funding for the engines. The prototype was to be produced under conditions of the utmost secrecy in Lockheed's Advanced Developments Projects Office, the engineering department of the Burbank factory known as the 'Skunk Works'. The name was derived from the 'Li'l Abner' cartoon strip character who brewed 'Kickapoo Joy Juice' in a shack from skunks, old boots and anything else that was handy, and was a hangover from 1943, when the XP-80 was being designed in makeshift workshops made from engine crates and circus tents adjacent to a foul-smelling plastics factory in Burbank.

The aircraft that emerged, known simply as CIA Article 341, was virtually a jet-powered sailplane with a slim fuselage, long tapered wings and a tall fin and rudder. It had a wingspan of 80 feet 2 inches and a length of 49 feet 8 inches and weighed 12,000 pounds empty, rising to 22,000 pounds take-off weight. It was powered by a 10,500-lbst Pratt & Whitney J57-PW-37 turbojet using a low-volatility, low vapour-pressure kerosene called JP-7. The cockpit featured a manually operated canopy that hinged to one side in the same way as the F-104's and there was no ejection seat. The camera compartment, or Q-bay, was installed in the fuselage immediately aft of the cockpit and was accessed via two doors, one in the fuselage spine, the other in the belly. The undercarriage comprised two tandem sets of twin wheels, those at the front being larger, and to balance the wings on take-off stanchions fitted with small dolly wheels called pogos were attached at mid-span. These dropped away as the aircraft became airborne and were reusable. Small skids were mounted on each wingtip.

While work progressed on the hand-built prototype – nicknamed the 'Angel' by the Lockheed staff – the Hycon Corporation of Southern California was also working on the camera system. The main camera, known as the Model 73B (or simply the Type B) was a revolutionary piece of equipment, incorporating a system that damped out engine vibration and compensated for the motion of the aircraft so that blurring would be eliminated, or as near as possible. It also allowed for the movement of Kodak's new, fast, highly sensitive film, which was wound on twin spools, each of which held about 6,000 feet and produced 4,000 pairs of stereoscopic photographs. The lens was the work of James G. Baker, the Harvard astronomer and optics expert who had done much pioneering work on camera optical systems in the Second World War. With a focal length of three feet and using thin low-grain film, it could produce photographs with a resolution of 60 lines per millimetre; this meant that 60 separate lines could be distinguished in every millimetre of a photograph taken at about 70,000 feet. In practical terms, the whole system could produce photographs which, when enlarged, could identify objects the size of a basketball shot from an altitude of 13 miles. Nor was that all; the system incorporated automatic lens focusing at all altitudes and a very advanced light meter that controlled the length of exposure depending on the light conditions in the target area. From 70,000 feet, the camera could cover a swathe of terrain up to 125 miles wide. The aircraft was not just a single-camera system however;

Kelly Johnson had designed it with adaptability in mind, so that during its career it could carry a variety of specialised cameras and sensors, as well as its own defensive ECM kit.

For testing the prototype, a site was selected at Groom Lake, which was part of the Atomic Energy Commission's nuclear test facility in the northwestern area of Nellis AFB. The site, nicknamed 'The Ranch', was ready by the summer of 1955, and on 24 July the prototype was split into its main component parts and ferried there in two C-124 Globemasters. At Groom, it was reassembled in a high-security hangar and prepared for taxi trials, the first of which was made by Lockheed test pilot Tony LeVier on 29 July. During the third taxi run, LeVier suddenly found himself airborne and cruising 35 feet above the runway. The aircraft showed no inclination to land and so he deliberately stalled it, hitting the runway hard. Both main wheel tyres blew, and the tail wheels suffered slight damage.

After repairs, LeVier took Article 341 on its official first flight on 1 August 1955. At the end of it he again found difficulty in landing, as the aircraft had a strong tendency to porpoise. In the end he made a full stall landing, and Article 341 settled gently on to the runway. All subsequent landings were made with the aircraft fully stalled, and great care had to be taken to keep it properly trimmed by balancing the fuel in the wing tanks. During the flight test phase, a technique was developed whereby a mobile control vehicle followed the aircraft down the runway, assisting the pilot by relaying his height above the surface. At the end of its landing roll the aircraft was allowed to settle on its wingtip skid; the ground crew would then attach the pogos so that the pilot could taxi in, in the normal manner.

The flight test programme showed that the U-2 – the aircraft had now been allocated a USAF designation – was a stable camera platform at all altitudes, but that flying it at its designed mission altitude required a great deal of care. Only a few knots separated a high speed buffet and a stall-induced buffet at very high altitude, and over-control produced an immediate pitching effect which, if not corrected smoothly and quickly, could result in the aircraft going out of control, followed by a catastrophic structural failure. It was a tendency that was to cost the life of more than one U-2 pilot.

Despite its unforgiving characteristics, the U-2 satisfactorily completed its test programme and the aircraft was ordered into production for the CIA, an initial contract calling for a batch of 20 aircraft under the designation U-2A. These were powered by an 11,200-lbst J57-P-31A engine and had a radar warning receiver in a tail cone. Early production aircraft were not fitted with ejection seats, although these were retrofitted at a later date when they became standard equipment on all U-2s. The U-2As were progressively delivered to Groom Lake, which became the main CIA U-2 operating base.

Five U-2As were modified for high-altitude air sampling, having an air intake mounted in the nose and and a forward-facing air scoop installed on the left side of the Q-bay, but the rest were assigned to the strategic reconnaissance role. There was now no longer any political obstacle to U-2 overflights of the Soviet Union going ahead; in July 1955 President Eisenhower had proposed his famous 'Open Skies' policy, which envisaged frequent inspection flights by US and Soviet reconnaissance aircraft over one another's territory and an exchange of information about military installations. The proposal followed hard on the heels of events at the 1955 Red Air Force Day at Tushino, Moscow, when western observers – including Colonel Charles E. Taylor, the US Air Attache in Moscow – had witnessed what appeared to be a whole wing of *Bison*

The Lockheed U-2 gave the Americans undreamed-of intelligence on the USSR's strategic capability. The aircraft shown is a later-model U-2R. (Colin Lambert)

strategic bombers in the flypast. It was a clever ruse; what the observers had seen was the same formation, deliberately varied in size, flying past several times. The inference, though, was that the *Bison* outnumbered its American counterpart, the Boeing B-52, by about four to one, so the position seemed grim. When the Soviet leadership, now under Nikita Khrushchev, rejected the Open Skies proposal out of hand, Eisenhower and his close advisers decided irrevocably that Operation *Overflight* would be set in motion.

By April 1956 the first group of U-2 pilots had completed their flight training and CIA indoctrination course, a rigorous procedure that included resistance to interrogation, survival techniques and personal endurance tests. Some pilots were ex-military; others were serving military personnel who had volunteered for special duties and were attached to the CIA in a temporary duty basis. The civilian pilots were 'employed' by Lockheed as 'flight test consultants', and various other cover stories were invented for the military participants.

The first four U-2 pilots to be declared operationally ready, together with the first two production U-2As, were deployed by Globemaster to RAF Lakenheath in Suffolk, the necessary approval having been given earlier in the year by senior RAF officers, senior officials of the British intelligence services, and Prime Minister Anthony Eden himself. For the benefit of curious aircraft spotters, who were bound to notice the U-2s when they carried out pre-mission test flights, the task of the Lockheed aircraft was stated to be high altitude weather reconnaissance, and the Lakenheath-based unit was given the cover designation of Weather Squadron (Provisional) One (WRSP-1).

The spotters lived up to their reputation, and from the moment the strange, unmarked aircraft made an appearance in British skies the country's aviation periodicals were deluged with letters from enthusiasts avid to know its identity and mission. For some time the USAF refused to comment, but it finally issued a statement to the effect that the machine was a Lockheed U-2 and that it was engaged in gathering information 'relating to clear air turbulence, convective clouds, wind shear and the jet stream...cosmic rays and the concentration of certain elements in the atmosphere, including ozone and water vapour'.

The spotters were not fooled. As the months passed there was a growing realisation that the mysterious U-2's activities might not be concerned solely with research, and that in some respects this strange machine, with its black anti-corrosion paint finish and total lack of identification markings, might be the proverbial wolf in sheep's clothing. In June 1957 the journal *Flying Review* ventured the opinion that 'it is possible that U-2s are flying across the Iron Curtain taking aerial photographs or probing radar defences'.

Flying Review had hit the nail squarely on the head, although by that time the U-2 detachment was no longer British-based and the overflights had been going on for a year. In June 1956, Anthony Eden had decided that U-2 operations from Britain would not be politically acceptable after all, and so WRSP-1 moved to Wiesbaden, Germany. Eden's decision was made in the light of a series of disastrous covert operations by the British Secret Intelligence Service, culminating in the mysterious death of the frogman Commander Lionel Crabbe in what was apparently an underwater mission to investigate sonar and other equipment on the Soviet cruiser *Sverdlov*, which was on a goodwill visit to Britain.

On 5 July 1956, after some preliminary high altitude flights over East Germany, U-2A Article 347 (USAF serial No. 56-6680) took off from Giebelstadt, a small airfield near the East–West German border, and headed for Moscow, where it photographed the Russian capital's defences and the nearby test airfield of Ramenskoye before turning north for Leningrad. A second mission to Leningrad was flown on 8 July. Both sorties were detected by the Russians' *Token* warning radars, but subsequent tracking was intermittent and inaccurate. On 9 July the Russians protested about the first flight, omitting to mention that the U-2 had overflown Moscow as well as Leningrad, and they made no reference at all to the 8 July mission. The protest note also described the aircraft that flew over Leningrad as 'twin-engined', which was probably a shot in the dark on the assumption that it was a PR Canberra. The US State Department naturally denied that a twin-engined American aircraft had been anywhere near Leningrad, but President Eisenhower was unhappy that the overflight had been picked up. While he understood that the U-2s were safe from interception, he saw the need for a future reconnaissance aircraft that would be truly 'invisible' to enemy defence systems. His awareness was to result in the launching of a research and development programme that would ultimately lead to a true 'stealth' aircraft.

In August 1956 a second CIA unit, WRSP-2, became operational at Incirlik air base near Adana, Turkey; it was also known by the CIA designation Detachment 10-10. In addition to overflights of the Soviet Union, the CIA authorised U-2 missions over the Middle East during the Suez Crisis of October–November 1956. These sorties were conducted in great secrecy. At 14.22 GMT on 6 November, a signal reached Allied Command in Cyprus from NATO Supreme Command in Europe that unidentified jet traffic, apparently heading for Syria or Egypt, had been detected passing through Turkish air space at high altitude. The Turkish Air Force was placed on full alert, and in the course of the afternoon RAF Hawker Hunter fighters from Nicosia were scrambled to investigate a suspicious radar contact 50 miles north of Cape Andreas. At a little over 50,000 feet, the Hunter pilots made contact with the suspect aircraft, which was several thousand feet above them, and made a positive identification. It was a U-2, operating out of Giebelstadt, on a mission to photograph the Cairo area and then recover to Incirlik. The operation was CIA-controlled, and the CIA had omitted to inform NATO what was happening. The photographs taken by the U-2s during the Suez Crisis were quickly made available to Allied Intelligence and proved of considerable use, but their importance has been exaggerated; it was the RAF Canberras and French RF-84Fs which brought back the photographic intelligence of real value. The important point about the exchange of information between the CIA and the Anglo-French Command was that it continued throughout the operation, despite severe differences at high political level.

In the summer of 1957 WRSP-1 joined its sister unit at Incirlik, the security of its main German operating base, Giebelstadt, having been compromised by Soviet Intelligence. In 1958 a third unit, WRSP-3, also became operational at Atsugi air base in Japan, from where it conducted overflights of the Soviet Far East, Korea and China.

It was in 1958 that the Royal Air Force became involved in the CIA's U-2 overflight programme. This move resulted from the adoption of a joint targeting policy by SAC and RAF Bomber Command; the RAF's V-bomber force was now a formidable deterrent in its own right, and the testing of British thermonuclear weapons in 1957 had helped to convince the USAF that Bomber Command would be a viable partner in a nuclear war. Indeed, the V-Force would be committed first, its bombers attacking Soviet targets several hours in advance of the main SAC force operating from the continental United States. Joint discussions revealed that every target on Bomber Command's list was also on SAC's, and that both Commands had doubled-up strikes on selected targets to ensure success, which was a waste of resources; moreover, Bomber Command's targets had hitherto been limited to Soviet airfields and naval bases presenting a direct threat to western Europe. Under the revised joint plan, Bomber Command would be allocated 69 cities which were centres of government or of other military significance; 17 long-range bomber airfields which constituted part of the nuclear threat; and 20 elements of the Soviet air defence system.

At this time, in late 1957 and early 1958, the CIA overflights were concentrating on the Soviet long-range missile test centres (Tyuratam, Kapustin Yar and Plesetsk) and the nuclear test sites in western Kazakhstan. The RAF's forthcoming U-2 mission would therefore be to photograph the strategic bomber bases. These included Chernyakhovsk, Tartu and Sol'tsy, south of the Baltic; Murmansk Northeast and Olenegorsk, on the Kola peninsula; Lvov, Bobruysk, Bykhov and Zhitomir, north of Kiev; Voronezh and Engels, in west-central Russia; and Saki, Adler and Oktyabr'skoya near the Black Sea, the latter being one of the penetration areas for V-bombers operating from Mediterranean bases.

The first batch of four RAF pilots assigned to the U-2 programme (Sqn Ldr Christopher Walker, and Flt Lts Michael Bradley, David Dowling and John MacArthur) were sent to Laughlin AFB, Texas, to undergo training in May 1958. Laughlin was a Strategic Air Command Base; SAC had taken delivery of its first U-2 (56-6696) there on 11 June 1957, the aircraft being assigned to the 4028th SRS of the 4080th SRW. The declared mission of SAC's U-2s was weather reconnaissance and atmospheric sampling, although – as we shall see later – they had a far wider role to play.

The RAF pilots went through the same stringent CIA indoctrination procedure as their American counterparts before beginning flight training. On 8 July 1958, Sqn Ldr Walker was killed when his U-2 broke up at high altitude, probably after going out of control, and crashed near Wayside, Texas; his place was taken by Flt Lt Robert Robinson, fresh from the British H-bomb trials at Christmas Island.

Speaking of British participation in the U-2 programme at a joint RAF/USAF historical seminar held in the USA in September 1993 (at which this author was also one of the speakers), Air Chief Marshal Sir Denis Smallwood, whose varied appointments included Commander-in-Chief UK Air Forces in 1975–6, commented that, '...It was held to be a matter of the highest security and very few people, certainly on the UK side, knew about it. We had four pilots for many years – they rotated, of course – based at Edwards AFB. From time to time, if I remember correctly, the U-2s would move forward into western Europe, particularly into Cyprus, and they would operate from there. I don't think – again, I am relying entirely on my memory here – that the RAF pilots ever actually conducted an operational sortie. The purpose of this bilateral agreement was that if the chips seemed to be down and one really needed to have a very wide-ranging reconnaissance programme using the U-2s, then the RAF pilots would be used. As far as the situation in Whitehall was concerned, as I have said, very few people were privy to this. The programme on the RAF side was run by the Assistant Chief of Air Staff (Operations) in the Ministry of Defence. It was a subject that came up occasionally during the Vice Chief to Vice Chief talks. It was certainly a subject talked about between the respective chiefs at that level and, of course, the Central Intelligence Agency and the Joint Intelligence Committee in London were involved. In London, it was certainly known to the Defence Committee at Cabinet level.'

Some sources, however, maintain that the RAF pilots were responsible for 'between two and four' of the 24 overflights that were made over the Soviet Union. Whatever the truth, it remains classified as this book is being written in the spring of 1997, and until the relevant documents are declassified it is quite useless to speculate. The official history of the U-2's operations has already been written by a US historian, but it cannot be released without the agreement of the British Government. If overflights conducted by RAF pilots had involved penetrations into Russia, it is hard to understand this attitude. But what if the RAF flights were made not over Russia, but over targets in other countries, particularly in the Middle East, which had been within the British sphere of influence but which were now leaning more and more towards the USSR and its doctrines? In some quarters, that might still have caused political embarrassment.

Most of the overflights of the Soviet Union were made in 1958–59; all were tracked and vigorous efforts were made to intercept them. Only the MiG-21 *Fishbed* fighter was capable of zoom-climbing to the U-2's operating altitude, and even then it was unable to manoeuvre. The Russian fighter squadrons were still equipped predominantly with the MiG-17 and MiG-19. The MiG-17PFU and the MiG-19PM were both armed with the AA-1 *Alkali* air-to-air missile, which operated in concert with the *Scan Odd* and *Spin Scan* AI radars, but the best they could do was to take 'snap shots' with it at the top of a zoom climb and the U-2 could easily avoid it as it reached the top of its trajectory. Moreover, the U-2As were now fitted with the *Sugar Scoop* infrared deflector, designed to lower the aircraft's infrared signature and shield it from AAMs fired from below.

In 1959 and the early months of 1960, although the number of operational sorties was now somewhat reduced, the CIA-operated U-2s turned their attention to Soviet IRBM and ICBM missile sites, and the intelligence they brought back was very revealing. The Americans had been seriously worried about the possibility that the Russians were deploying large numbers of ICBMs, especially after the launch of *Sputnik 1* – the first artificial earth satellite – in October 1957, but U-2 photographs and reconnaissance by first-generation satellites showed that no more than four had been deployed. The ICBM in question was the SS-6 *Sapwood*, which never materialised as a viable weapon system.

In April 1960, however, the CIA received information that the Russians were developing what appeared to be a very advanced missile site near Sverdlovsk, and a U-2 of Detachment 10-10 was detailed to photograph it, together with the missile test centre at Tyuratam and the air and naval bases at Archangelsk and Murmansk. The aircraft selected for the mission was a U-2B (serial No. 56-6693). The U-2B was a modified U-2A, one of seven fitted with the 15,800-lbst Pratt & Whitney J75-P-13A engine; range, payload and airframe fatigue life were all extended, and the aircraft was internally strengthened to accept the higher thrust and increased weight of the new engine.

At the end of April 56-6693 was deployed from Incirlik to Peshawar in Pakistan. Most overflights took place from this location, as traffic from Incirlik was heavily monitored by the Russians. This particular U-2 was not a favourite aircraft among Detachment 10-10's pilots, who had encountered fuel transfer problems while changing from one tank to another in the air. Nevertheless, it was the only U-2 that could be spared for the mission, so at 06.26 local time on the morning of 1 May 1960 it took off from Peshawar and climbed out over northern Afghanistan on the first leg of a nine-hour, 2,800-mile flight over the Soviet Union that would terminate at nightfall on the NATO air base of Bodo, in northern Norway. It was the first time that a U-2 mission had been planned to fly across the full breadth of the Soviet Union; it was also the first U-2 overflight to take place on communism's traditional day of celebration.

The U-2's pilot was a civilian employee of the CIA. His name was Francis Gary Powers.

12

The 'U-2 Incident'

BY THE TIME Powers' U-2 crossed into Soviet territory it was flying at an altitude of 68,000 feet. Powers went up another couple of thousand feet, levelled out and switched over to the automatic pilot, noting that the outside air temperature was −60°C. Below the aircraft stretched an unbroken bank of cloud, not of particular significance from the reconnaissance point of view at this stage of the flight, for there was nothing much of interest on the surface. When the cloud layer finally ended the pilot found himself more or less on track, south-east of the Aral Sea.

Looking down, Powers picked out a condensation trail, arrow-straight across the dark earth and on a reciprocal heading to his own. The aircraft at its head was travelling very fast, possibly at supersonic speed, but it was a long way below and it quickly vanished. A few minutes later another contrail appeared, this time travelling in the same direction as the U-2, but this aircraft too remained far below and Powers eventually lost it.

Baikonur Cosmodrome – the space centre from which, a year later, Yuri Gagarin would blast off to become the first man in orbit – lay on the U-2's track, and although it was not a primary target on the U-2's itinerary it had been decided to include it anyway, as information returned by earlier U-2 flights had proved disappointing. Powers therefore rolled his cameras as he passed over Baikonur before flying on towards Chelyabinsk. The clouds had dispersed completely now, and the snow-capped Ural Mountains were clearly visible, running like a great jagged scar from north to south, cutting through green landscape on either side.

Suddenly, the U-2's nose pitched sharply upwards in the dangerous porpoising motion that all U-2 pilots had learned to anticipate and cope with. Powers quickly disengaged the autopilot and took over manual control, trimming the aircraft for level flight before engaging the autopilot again. The U-2 flew on for about ten minutes and then the nose pitched up again, leaving Powers no choice but to revert to manual control. The fact that he would have to pilot the aircraft manually for the rest of the sortie was by no means a disaster, but it would add considerably to his workload, and he would need all his concentration for the task of monitoring the U-2's reconnaissance systems. He was now about 1,300 miles deep into Russia and the weather conditions ahead of him were perfect.

The U-2's next objective was Sverdlovsk, an important industrial centre which was of special interest to US Intelligence because of some curious domed structures, believed to be missile silos, which were reported to be under construction in the vicinity. So far, no U-2 flight had been made over the area. From Sverdlovsk, Powers was briefed to continue to Plesetsk, another missile test centre in the north. Thirty miles south of Sverdlovsk, the pilot made a turn to the left and settled down on a new heading that would take him over the strange installations and the south-west suburb of the town. He had now been airborne for four hours.

As he ran in towards his target, Powers detected an airfield which was not marked on his map, and he logged its position carefully. At that moment, he sensed rather than heard a dull explosion and a vivid orange glare enveloped his aircraft, which lurched violently. The U-2 had in fact been near-missed by an SA-2 *Guideline* surface-to-air missile, one of a salvo of 14 launched at the high-flying aircraft. Powers was unlucky in that the battery had only recently been established near Sverdlovsk.

It seemed an age, Powers wrote later, before the orange light died away. The U-2's right wing began to sink and he moved the control column over to the left, levelling the aircraft again. Then the U-2's nose dropped, and this time the controls failed to respond. An instant later, a fearful vibration shook the aircraft as both wings tore away. The weight of the engine dragged the tail down and Powers found himself lying on his back. The fuselage began to spin and the 'g' forces pinned him to his seat.

The U-2's cockpit was small, the pilot sitting with his legs stretched out in a kind of tunnel beneath the instrument panel. The layout was much the same as that of a high-performance glider, but it meant that before he could eject, the U-2 pilot had to move his seat back on its rails and pull his legs clear of the panel. Powers pulled the lever that moved the seat, but it refused to budge. Quite simply, this meant that if he attempted to eject now, he would lose both legs a few inches above the knee as he left the cockpit.

The only other alternative was to bale out in the orthodox manner. A glance at the altimeter showed him that the U-2, still spinning wildly, was already below 35,000 feet and falling at an alarming rate. He pulled the canopy jettison handle, and almost instantly the faceplate of his pressure helmet frosted over. He unfastened his seat harness, then remembered that he was supposed to activate the U-2's destruct mechanism. If he had ejected this would have happened automatically, but now he had to throw a red-painted switch on the starboard side of the cockpit. He groped for it, unable to see because of his iced-up faceplate, but failed to locate it and decided to concentrate all his efforts on saving himself. He tried to lever himself out of the cockpit, but something pulled him up sharply and there was a moment of panic before he remembered that he had not unclipped his oxygen lead. He tore it free, and a moment later he and the tumbling fuselage parted company.

Powers' parachute opened automatically at 15,000 feet and he landed in a ploughed field close to a Russian village. The rest is history. His subsequent interrogation and trial made worldwide headlines, and the U-2 incident effectively wrecked a major East–West summit conference which was scheduled to be held in Paris a fortnight later. Powers himself was sentenced to ten years' imprisonment in the Soviet Union, but after serving two years he was exchanged for the Russian spy Colonel Rudolf Abel.

The Powers incident brought an end to overflights of the Soviet Union, and all U-2 operations and aircraft were gradually shifted to the US Air Force. In the Far East, U-2 overflights of China continued, the aircraft being flown by Chinese Nationalist pilots; in September and October 1962 two of them were shot down, one by a fighter and the other by an SA-2 missile. In the following year, four U-2s were supplied to the Chinese Nationalist Air Force, and all four of them were subsequently destroyed on operations.

Meanwhile, the U-2 had proved its worth in arming the United States with vital intelligence on serious events in Cuba, an island where the regime of Fidel Castro had brought the Soviet brand of Marxism to the very doorstep of North America.

13

The Cuban Crisis

BOTH CIA AND Air Force U-2s had been monitoring Cuba ever since 1959, when Fidel Castro had become premier after overthrowing the pro-American government of President Batista. On 29 August 1962, a CIA U-2 returned with photographic evidence that SA-2 *Guideline* SAM sites were being built on the island. The presence of Russian-built MiG-21 interceptors on Cuban airfields had already been noted, and at first sight it might have been thought that the SA-2s were merely the second component of a new and modern air defence system being installed by the Russians. But SA-2 sites had been photographed in the Soviet Union, and the CIA photo interpreters knew that they followed set patterns, depending on the kind of target they were designed to defend. For example, SA-2 sites in the shape of a trapezoid were designed to protect nuclear weapons storage bunkers, medium and intermediate range ballistic missile complexes, shipyards and bomber bases.

As the weeks went by, the evidence began to accumulate that the Russians were up to something in Cuba. Russian freighters heading from the Black Sea to Havana carried mysterious crates that might contain Ilyushin Il-28 jet bombers or even strategic missiles. Armed with this alarming information, President John F. Kennedy ordered the overflights to be stepped up, although each one must have presidential approval. The flights were also to be conducted by Strategic Air Command pilots, rather than CIA; the thinking was that if a U-2 were to be shot down over Cuba during any forthcoming hostilities, its pilot would be treated as a legitimate prisoner of war.

On Sunday, 14 October 1962, two U-2s of the 4080th Strategic Reconnaissance Wing took off from McCoy AFB in Florida and headed for Cuba. Flown by Majors Rudolf Anderson, Jr, and Richard S. Heyser, the aircraft were U-2Es; the E model was a U-2A airframe fitted with a J75-P-13B engine, giving it extra altitude, and additional ECM equipment mounted in pods on the tail and a small fairing on top of the fuselage.

The U-2s were assigned different sectors, and it was Heyser, photographing the San Cristobal area, who came back with the evidence that proved beyond all doubt that the Russians were preparing to deploy medium- and intermediate-range ballistic missiles to Cuba. The photographs revealed missile transporters, erector-launchers, control bunkers, vehicle revetments, oxidizer and propellant trucks, tented and prefabricated accommodation, and large mounds of earth that clearly concealed nuclear warhead storage bunkers.

The missiles were identified as the SS-4 *Sandal* MRBM, which had a range of around 1,250 miles and was the first Soviet missile to use storable liquid fuel. The

Although U-2s provided much coverage of the missile buildup in Cuba, the bulk of the PR task was carried out by reconnaissance versions of the F-8 Crusader and the F-101 Voodoo.

IRBM was the SS-5 *Skean*, which had a range of around 2,000 miles. Both missiles had their drawbacks in operational use, their launch process involving an enormous amount of time and effort. The SS-4 needed about eight hours preparation time before firing, and the SS-5 could only be maintained at a state of readiness for five hours.

The air reconnaissance effort over Cuba was dramatically intensified, the U-2s of the 4080th SRW overflying the island 102 times between 14 October and 16 December 1962. Low-level reconnaissance sorties over Cuba were also made by RF-101 Voodoos of the 363rd Tactical Reconnaissance Wing from Shaw AFB in South Carolina and by RF-8A Crusaders of the US Navy's Light Photographic Squadron 26. Three U-2s were lost during these operations. One of them, flown by Major Rudolf Anderson, was shot down over the naval base at Banes by an SA-2 missile on 27 October and its pilot killed; the others disappeared in unknown circumstances. Also on 27 October, an RB-47 of the 55th SRW, one of the many aircraft engaged in searching for Russian cargo vessels carrying arms to Cuba, crashed on take-off at Kindley AFB, Bermuda, killing all four crew.

At 19.00 hr eastern standard time on 22 October, President Kennedy, in a televised speech lasting 17 minutes, announced to an unsuspecting American public the discovery of Russian missiles in Cuba and the immediate imposition of a naval blockade around the island. As the President began to speak, American forces worldwide were placed on a higher state of alert, with SAC moving to Defense Condition (DEFCON) Three. Battle staffs were placed on 24-hour alert duty, leaves cancelled and personnel recalled. B-47s were dispersed to several widely separated and pre-selected civilian and military airfields, additional bombers and tankers were placed on ground alert, and the B-52 airborne alert indoctrination programme was immediately expanded into an actual airborne alert involving 24-hour sorties by armed aircraft and the immediate replacement in the air of each aircraft that landed. SAC's ICBM force, at that time numbering about 200 operational missiles, was brought into alert configuration.

As the crisis developed, the US intelligence agencies believed they had identified 24 SS-4 launchers, of which 20 were fully operational; the remaining four were expected to be operational early in November. The photographic interpreters had positively identified 33 SS-4 missiles at San Cristobal and Sagua la Grande, but were of the opinion that there were probably more, while a third site at Guanajay, north of San Cristobal, was apparently being readied to receive SS-5s. The first four SS-5 launchers were expected to be operational by 1 December, and the second and third SS-5 groups by the 15th. A fourth SS-5 group was clearly planned and construction of the site had begun. In fact, delivery of the last six SS-4s (of which there were actually 42 planned for deployment) and all 32 SS-5s was blocked by the naval quarantine. No MRBM or IRBM nuclear warheads were ever identified in Cuba, but a Soviet artillery battalion equipped with *Frog* tactical rockets was present on the island, and it was revealed many years later that the missiles were nuclear-tipped and that its commander had the discretion to use them in the event of an American invasion.

Had war come, the spearhead of an attack on the Soviet facilities in Cuba would have been the Republic F-105 Thunderchiefs of Tactical Air Command's 4th Tactical Fighter Wing, which deployed to MaCoy AFB on 21 October. The 4th TFW began a one-hour alert status at 04.00 hr the next day, and this was reduced to 15 minutes in the afternoon. But the F-105s were held back while international negotiations proceeded, and when they flew it was in the air defence role, patrolling the southern Florida peninsula on the lookout for Il-28 jet bombers. Nevertheless, TAC's RF-101 sorties made certain that the fighter-bombers' target folders were kept updated on a regular basis. In Europe, which would certainly have been the first to feel an armed Soviet backlash against any armed American action in Cuba, the nuclear alert force comprised USAF F-100 Super Sabre tactical fighter bombers deployed on British bases, backed up by Thor IRBMs deployed with the RAF in the United Kingdom, and RAF Valiant bombers armed with tactical nuclear weapons of American origin.

By the morning of 24 October a formidable naval blockading force was in place on the approaches to Cuba. At its heart was Task Force 136, comprising seventeen destroyers, two cruisers, the attack carriers *Enterprise* and *Independence* and the anti-submarine carriers *Randolph* and *Essex*. In all, 480 ships were involved in the operation. A quarantine arc was established 500 miles north-east of Cuba and US Navy surveillance aircraft, both carrier- and shore-based, ensured that nothing entered it without being detected. When a ship was detected it was stopped, allowed to proceed if its cargo was innocuous, and turned back if it was not.

On 25 October, with no sign of an easing of tension, American forces worldwide went to DEFCON Two. On the 27th, there occurred an incident which might have had serious consequences, when a U-2 of the 4080th SRW flown by Major Charles Maultsby and genuinely engaged in a scientific flight to measure radiation in the upper atmosphere between Alaska and the North Pole, inadvertently strayed over cloud into Soviet air space. To the Russian air defence radar controllers, this must have seemed

If the USA had gone to war over Cuba, attacks on the Soviet IRBM and MRBM sites would have been made by Tactical Air Command's F-105 Thunderchiefs.

like a last-minute reconnaissance flight preceding an attack on Soviet air bases in the Anadyr area, and fighters were scrambled to intercept it. American radar in Alaska alerted Maultsby to the danger and he swung round in a 45-degree turn towards the coast, breaking radio silence with a call for help on what pilots wryly know as the OMG (Oh My God) frequency. His call was answered by a flight of Convair F-102 Delta Daggers, which made rendezvous with the U-2 over the Bering Sea and escorted it to the safety of an Alaskan airfield.

Also on 27 October (a Saturday) there was an indication that the RAF was about to become involved in the quarantine when Nos 42, 201 and 206 Squadrons, RAF Coastal Command at St Mawgan in Cornwall, were alerted for a deployment to the Caribbean. All three squadrons, which were armed with the Avro Shackleton and had an offensive anti-submarine role, were ready to deploy to Bermuda when their mission was cancelled at the last moment. The exact nature of that mission is still not clear, but in a report on the deployment and status of forces during the Cuban Missile Crisis, the US Joint Chiefs of Staff stated that 'aircraft from Bermuda and Roosevelt Roads, Puerto Rico, will conduct daylight searches to the East of the Quarantine Arc. Additional land based patrol aircraft are being provided by COMASWFORLANT (Commander, Antisubmarine Warfare Force, Atlantic) from Bermuda and Roosevelt Roads.' As Bermuda was a dependent British colony, this statement implied that either the UK Government had given permission for the use of its airfields by US forces, or that British maritime aircraft were taking an active part in the quarantine.

On 28 October, Premier Khrushchev agreed to the withdrawal of all offensive missiles from Cuba, subject to verification by the United Nations. It was the first major break in the crisis. Throughout the next few days, SAC reconnaissance aircraft – U-2s and RB-47s – maintained close aerial surveillance while the missiles were dismantled, loaded on ships, and sent back through the quarantine to the USSR.

On 20 November, when the Russians agreed to move their Il-28 medium bombers from Cuba, the quarantine was lifted and the air and naval forces began shifting back to normal operations. In SAC, the B-47 medium bombers returned to their home bases, the ground alert force dropped back to the normal 50 per cent standard, and routine B-52 airborne alert indoctrination flights recommenced.

Six days later, during a visit to Homestead AFB, Florida, President Kennedy presented the Air Force Outstanding Unit Award to the 4080th Strategic Reconnaissance Wing for its reconnaissance effort over Cuba.

14

Reconnaissance and ECM in Support of the RAF V-Bomber Force

ON 1 JUNE 1955, RAF Bomber Command's strategic reconnaissance capability was transformed almost overnight with the re-formation of No. 543 Squadron at RAF Gaydon, Warwickshire. In November it began moving to RAF Wyton under the command of Wg Cdr R. E. Havercroft, and by April 1956 it had an establishment of ten Vickers Valiant B(PR).1 aircraft. In the day role, the PR Valiant carried up to eight

Vickers Valiant B(PR)1 WZ392 clearly shows the positioning of the bomb bay cameras.

main F96 fan cameras with 48-in lenses to provide horizon-to-horizon cover, and a tri-installation of three F49 wide-angle survey cameras, all – with the exception of two of the wide-angle cameras – mounted in a camera crate in the bomb bay. Behind this, in a fairing, was another F49 survey camera, with the two oblique cameras of the wide-angle installation mounted above it. In the night role, the B(PR).1 carried five or six cameras in the camera crate, together with five or six photo-cell units. Photo-flashes were housed in a flash crate at the rear of the bomb bay.

On 9 February 1956, at which time it had five Valiants on strength, No. 543 Squadron made its first serious contribution to V-Force activity when it took part in a Bomber Command V-Force interception trial, providing two aircraft out of a total force of seven Valiants and 18 Canberras. The purpose of the trial was to conduct a study of V-Force penetration and interception problems and to observe the degree of success that the fighters and radar defences had in dealing with the penetration. The squadron ORB records that 'both of the aircraft provided completed the briefed route, according to plan'.

With its crews only just emerging from the operational conversion unit phase, No. 543 Squadron was not yet qualified to take up its photographic task. Instead, it busied itself with continuation training; in March 1956 it carried out a Continental cross-country training exercise for the first time, and in May it flew six sorties in the Bomber Command Exercise *Rejuvenate*, the purpose of which was to give Fighter Command aircraft interception practice in the sector covering the northwest approaches to the UK. On 24 June Wg Cdr Havercroft took one of No. 543's Valiants (WZ394) to Idris in Libya to take part in Exercise *Thunderhead*, designed to test NATO defences in the north-eastern Mediterranean. Another 543 Squadron Valiant spent the summer of 1956 carrying out trials with *Yellow Aster*, which was the code name for the H2S Mk 9, a non-scanning radar system designed to make it possible to carry out all-weather reconnaissance operations.

The Valiants were not yet fully equipped for their specialised reconnaissance role, and during 1956 aircraft were sent to Vickers-Armstrongs Ltd, Weybridge, and Marshall's Ltd of Cambridge, for modification, but as the fully-modified aircraft were returned to the squadron a series of seven-hour cross-country flights was initiated for general research into flight planning, fuel loading and aircraft performance. From 9 October to 29 December 1956 two Valiants were detached to RCAF Namao, near Edmonton, Alberta, to assess the effect of winter conditions on airborne radar equipment. Further phases of this exercise, called Operation *Snow Trip*, followed early in 1957; all the flying was directly concerned with radar coverage of various targets obtained from different heights with both radial and Sidescan radar.

In May 1957 No. 543 Squadron conducted its first operational reconnaissance during Exercise *Vigilant*, two crews flying each night to carry out radar targeting raids. Four very successful sorties were completed, and in June two Valiants went to Malta to give a demonstration of their equipment and operating techniques to representatives of Allied Forces Mediterranean (AFMED). Prior to the presentation, the Valiants flew several special Sidescan sorties; details are not specified, but the sorties may have involved flights to the Black Sea area.

Two of No. 543 Squadron's crews were now declared 'combat' classified. The crews concerned were those of Wg Cdr Havercroft and Sqn Ldr G. D. Cremer (who, it will be recalled, had taken part in the RAF RB-45C sorties over the USSR some years earlier).

Much of No. 543 Squadron's operational task involved photomapping to provide necessary data for the inertial navigation system of the Avro Blue Steel stand-off missile, seen here with its loading apparatus.

It was Sqn Ldr Cremer who commanded a detachment of two Valiants (WZ391 and WZ392) that went to RAAF Edinburgh Field, South Australia, in August 1957 to participate in Operation *Antler*, a series of British nuclear tests at the Maralinga Range. Three nuclear explosions were involved, on 14 and 25 September and on 9 October 1957, the purpose of the trials being to gather information about the triggering mechanism (fission primary) for the thermonuclear bombs that were soon to be tested at Christmas Island. (In fact, *Antler* Round 2, code-named *Indigo Hammer*, involved a 6-kiloton device that could also be used as a warhead for the Bloodhound surface-to-air missile.) During the trials, the Valiants carried out photographic and radar reconnaissance before, during and after each test.

During the detachment, the Valiants also flew three radar reconnaissance sorties on behalf of the Weapon Research Establishment, gathering data in connection with the Avro Blue Steel stand-off missile project. Chosen to arm the Vulcans and Victors of the V-Force, Blue Steel had an interesting three-part aircraft/missile guidance and control system comprising an inertial navigator, flight rules computer and autopilot. The navigator computed the present position of the missile; the flight rules computer (FRC) determined the flight plan, and the autopilot commanded the control movements necessary to obtain the desired flight path. During the captive phase of the flight, Blue Steel's navigation system was coupled with that of the parent aircraft, providing additional information to the crew on their position and also, by comparing data from fixed positions along the route, allowing corrections to be fed into the missile. Because the aircraft/missile navigational system relied on very accurate position fixing on the

Handley Page Victor B/SR Mk 2s of No. 543 Squadron at RAF Wyton.

run-up to weapon release, the navigational charts used by Bomber Command had to be updated and, if necessary, modified to rule out any slight errors. Before Blue Steel became operational, therefore, large areas of the earth's surface were photographically mapped by No. 543 Squadron's Valiants, and this activity accounted for much of the squadron's task between 1957 and 1962.

In 1964, three Valiants and four crews of No. 543 Squadron were positioned at Salisbury Airport, Southern Rhodesia, for Operation *Pontifex*. This involved an aerial survey of Northern and Southern Rhodesia and Bechuanaland. The operation was under the control of the Central Reconnaissance Establishment and was believed to be the largest task of this nature ever undertaken by the RAF, covering 400,000 square miles of territory. During the operation, Valiant WZ394 developed a crack in the rear wing spar and had to return to the UK for repair. It was a foretaste of troubles to come; when other Valiants were inspected more indications of metal fatigue were discovered, and the whole Valiant force was withdrawn from operational service in January 1965.

As far as No. 543 Squadron was concerned, the consequences were more immediate. Inspections of its aircraft showed that only one was fit to fly a limited number of hours; six of the remaining seven were available for emergency use only, to be serviced and made ready for combat as required.

Plans had already been laid for the PR Valiants to be replaced by the Handley Page Victor B/SR MK 2 in 1967, but the premature withdrawal of the Valiant meant that the Victor had to be phased into the reconnaissance role sooner than planned. Work was accelerated on the prototype PR Victor, XL165, and this was flown at Radlett on 23

A Vulcan B.2 (MRR) of No. 617 Squadron on maritime patrol over the North Sea. The aircraft has not yet received its full ECM fit.

February 1965, being delivered to the A&AEE at Boscombe Down for acceptance trials in March. The second SR.2 conversion was XM718, which had been rebuilt following a crash landing at RAF Wittering; this aircraft also went to Boscombe Down and was eventually delivered to No. 543 Squadron in January 1966. The squadron's first SR.2 was XL230, which was delivered to Wyton on 19 May 1965. Two Victors were on strength by June, four by September, five by November and six by January 1966. The eleventh and last aircraft was delivered on 21 June 1966; unfortunately, just a few days later, while carrying out a low-level demonstration for the benefit of Press photographers on 29 June, SR.2 XM716 broke up in mid-air and crashed at Warboys with the loss of its crew. It was being flown by Sq Ldr J. A. Holland, who had captained the first of 543's crews to convert to the Victor.

In terms of operational effectiveness, the Victor had many advantages over the earlier Valiant. It had a better altitude and speed, and its range was 40 per cent greater. For day photography, it carried a battery of F96 Mk 2 cameras; for night work, the F89 Mk 3; and for survey and mapping, the F49 Mk 4. Three bomb bay canisters could accommodate 108 eight-inch photo flashes, each of several million candlepower. One Victor SR.2 could photograph the whole Mediterranean in a single seven-hour sortie, bringing back 10,000 feet of exposed film for processing either at Wyton or at the Joint Air Reconnaissance Intelligence Centre at nearby RAF Brampton; infrared false-colour film proved particularly effective, giving a more effective penetration of camouflage than infra-red black and white. Five Victors could cover the whole of the Atlantic in less than seven hours.

Maritime Radar Reconnaissance, in fact, was one of No. 543 Squadron's priority tasks, developed operationally during the Valiant days; in September 1965 the squadron flew three maritime co-operation exercises, and the task became increasingly important as the Russians continued to develop and extend their new long-range ocean-going naval forces. It was a role that No. 543 continued to exercise until its disbandment on 24 May 1974, the operational task having been taken over by the Vulcan B.2 (MRR) aircraft of No. 27 Squadron.

On 30 September 1957, while No. 543 Squadron's Valiants were taking part in the atomic weapons trials in Australia, No. 199 Squadron re-formed at RAF Honington with Valiants in the specialist electronic countermeasures role. During the Second World War the squadron had operated as a unit of No. 100 Group in the bomber support role until disbandment in July 1945. It had re-formed in the same role as part of the Central Signals Establishment at Watton, flying Lincoln Mk2/4As and Mosquito NF.36s, but on 17 April 1952 it was transferred from No. 90 (Signals) Group to Bomber Command, becoming a squadron in No. 1 Group. Its main flying task initially was to provide radio countermeasures training for Fighter and Anti-Aircraft Commands, 39 hours and 20 hours respectively being allocated to these two Commands per month; 18 hours of the operational flying task were devoted to Bomber Command, and eleven to the Royal Navy. Early in 1954, when the Mosquitos were at last retired, the squadron's establishment was nine Lincolns and one Canberra B.2.

After No. 199 Squadron's re-formation at Honington, the Lincolns and the Canberra were assigned to No. 1321 Flight at Hemswell. The Flight remained operational in the ECM role from 1 October 1957 until 31 March 1958, by which time its strength had been reduced to two Lincoln B.2s, the Canberra having been transferred to Honington.

The Valiant had not been designed to accommodate an ECM fit, and many modifications were necessary before the first aircraft was ready for service with No. 199 Squadron. The operational ECM Valiants were equipped with APT-16A and ALT-7 jamming transmitters, *Airborne Cigar* and *Carpet-4* jammers, APR9 and APR4 search receivers, and *Window* dispensers. Compatibility trials were carried out by a 'special' Valiant, WP214, at the Bomber Command Development Unit, Finningley; the onboard equipment generated intense heat, and special cooling systems had to be devised and installed. The jamming transmitters were contained in nine separate cylindrical drums, each about 3 feet high, 18 inches in diameter and weighing 200 pounds. They covered the metric and centimetric wavebands and were intended to jam enemy ground radar and air-to-air radio and radar. The whole kit was cooled by a water/glycol system consisting of an elaborate configuration of pipes connected to a special air intake and heat exchanger. Other items of equipment in the modified Valiants included a passive warning receiver system to alert the crew when ground radar was locked on to their aircraft, an active tail warning receiver, a turbo-alternator to provide the AC power necessary to operate the jamming equipment, and five separate sets of aerials connected with the ECM apparatus, situated in the nose, tail, both wingtips and beneath the fuselage. The special Valiants carried two air electronics operators and one navigator.

Bomber Command envisaged that the rearming of No. 199 Squadron with the Valiant would cover a minimum of nine months, the aircraft being progressively delivered as they were modified for the ECM role. The squadron's function was to introduce ECM techniques to the V-Force, and once this requirement had been achieved No. 199 Squadron disbanded on 15 December 1958, its 'C' Flight going to

Finningley to form the nucleus of a re-formed No. 18 Squadron, which – eventually armed with six Valiants – would now provide ECM support for the whole of the V-Force.

In retrospect, it is doubtful whether the squadron would have proved very effective under war conditions, for six Valiants could hardly have provided an effective ECM screen for the entire V-Force. In addition, the jamming equipment was subject to severe limitations in that it could only cover a very narrow frequency band at any one time, and even then the jamming transmissions were only at their best when the aircraft flew port side on to the stations that were being jammed.

The real solution to the problem was for the spearhead aircraft of the V-Force, the Mk.2 versions of the Vulcan and Victor, to carry their own ECM equipment; this had not been possible with the first-generation V-bombers because too much space was taken up by the bulky navigation/bombing system (NBS). The requirement for the installation of ECM in the V-bombers had already been defined in December 1956, in a paper prepared by the Operational Requirements Branch. The paper acknowledged that Russian defences were becoming increasingly effective against subsonic bombers, predicting that:

> 'These defences will become extremely lethal to the V-Force in three or four years' time unless methods of reducing their efficiency are devised and the aircraft appropriately fitted... Some increase in safety can be achieved if the aircraft are developed to give improved performance – in speed and height in order to stretch the interception procedures and in range to give the opportunity to employ evasive routeing where possible. There is, however, a limit to these improvements which is set by basic aircraft design parameters and therefore other expedients must be employed to keep down the loss rate. It is generally accepted that defensive armament is not profitable in present concepts where air-to-air and surface-to-air weapons will ultimately constitute the most serious threat to the bombers.'

As an interesting aside, the writer of this paper does not seem to have envisaged low-level operations as a means of penetrating enemy defences. Yet a specially-strengthened, low-level version of the Valiant, the B.Mk.2, had flown in 1953; it could reach a maximum speed at sea level of 552 mph, whereas the B.1 was limited by airframe considerations to 414 mph. In the mid-1950s, however, the Air Staff had decided that there was not a requirement for it, and the sole prototype was scrapped.

The paper went on to describe the Russian air defence radar that was in place at the time.

> 'The principal ground radar in the Russian C and R (control and reporting) system is the *Token* centimetric (S band) equipment. It is a multi-beam, continuous height-finding radar operating on five or seven frequencies... It is backed up by a chain of metric stations, most of which are now of the *Kniferest* type operating on 65 to 75 mc/s with apparently the additional ability to operate on frequencies up to about 104 mc/s as an anti-jamming measure. The Russians seem clearly aware of the vulnerability of these radars to jamming.
>
> The Russian fighter control operates in the conventional VHF band between 100 and 156 mc/s. The aircraft equipment is a simple four-channel set which rather restricts the flexibility of control. This suggests that the control may be

fairly vulnerable to countermeasures despite the possibility of using a substantial high-power transmitter on the ground as a countermeasure step.

Although it is realised that with alternative frequencies ground radars can be used to supplement the *Token* and *Kniferest* stations, it would take a considerable time for even the Russians to provide comprehensive cover on new frequencies. In any case, it would be very difficult to cloak such intentions from our intercept service; the same considerations apply, but to a lesser degree, to a possible change from VHF to UHF fighter communications.'

An analysis of the Russian electronic defences resulted in the development of three types of jammer for use in the second-generation V-bombers. These were the ARI 18076 centimetric jammer, the ARI 18074 communications jammer, and the ARI 18075 metric jammer. In the case of the third of the V-bombers, the Victor, the necessary modifications to accommodate this equipment were relatively uncomplicated, as most of it could be fitted into the existing area of the rear fuselage. With the Vulcan it was a different story because it meant that the whole of the rear fuselage had to be redesigned to accommodate the new equipment, and Avro suddenly received the instruction to incorporate it when the Vulcan B.2 development programme was well under way.

As well as the ECM equipment mentioned above, the new fit included a tail warning radar known as *Red Steer*, developed by the Telecommunications Research Establishment at Malvern from an AI13 set, which had been standard equipment in the

This photograph of Vulcan B.2 XM646 landing at RAF Waddington shows the redesigned rear fuselage, accommodating the ECM equipment, and the ECM fairing on the tail fin.

A close-up of the ECM fairings on a Vulcan B.2 (MRR) of No. 27 Squadron.

Meteor NF11/NF14 night-fighter. USAF Strategic Air Command's ECM kit was more sophisticated, but also a good deal more expensive, and what would fit into a B-52 certainly would not fit into a Vulcan or Victor. In any case, the RAF's argument was that the key to successful ECM was to prevent an enemy fighter from attaining visual contact with the bomber he was meant to destroy, which in turn meant blocking the VHF frequencies used to guide him to his target, and noise jamming was as good as, if not better than, many other more costly methods. The four Soviet VHF channels in use during the late 1950s were well monitored, and all could be jammed by the ARI 18074 *Green Palm*, which like the wartime *Jostle* used by No. 100 Group emitted a high-pitched wail. The Soviet fighters of the late 1950s also carried a device, developed from the German *Naxos*-Z of 1944, which enabled them to home on to transmissions from blind bombing radars such as H2S, so the H2S Mk 9A carried by the Vulcan and Victor incorporated a modification known as *Fishpool*, which enabled the radar navigator to detect enemy fighters below and, to some extent, on either side of the aircraft.

To accommodate the new ECM gear, the Vulcan Mk 2 sprouted a new tail cone, increasing the overall length by 2 feet 10 inches, and a flat aerial plate was fitted between the two starboard jet pipes. The rear fuselage bulge first appeared on the second B.2, XH534, which flew in 1959 and spent seven years on trials work with the A&AEE before being delivered to No. 230 OCU in December 1966.

By that time, the Mk.2 V-bombers were fully operational; the services of No. 18

The BAC TSR-2, cancelled in 1965, would have had a formidable reconnaissance capability at all altitudes. It was to have replaced the Canberra in the strike/reconnaissance roles.

Squadron had not been required for some time and it had disbanded in 1963, re-forming later as a helicopter squadron. The whole of the V-Force had now gone over to low-level operations, and in this new role the Vulcans and Victors carried four types of ECM fit. As well as the ARI 18074, 18075 and 18076 jammers, the ARI 5919 *Red Steer* active tail warning receiver (later replaced by the ARI 5952) and the ARI 18105 passive warning receiver (to warn when a ground radar was locked on), they also carried the 18205 L-band radar jammer, the 18146 X-band jammer (in the Victors) and the 18051, a system for dispensing rapid blooming *Window* and/or infrared decoy flares developed by Microcell Ltd.

Fortunately, Bomber Command was never called upon to put its ECM equipment to the test in a real war situation; but the many exercises in which the V-bombers participated proved beyond all doubt that many of them would have got through to their targets in what would have swiftly become the nuclear ruin of the Northern Hemisphere. And it is a sobering thought that the Air Staff always anticipated that the V-Force, rapidly degrading through combat losses and the destruction of its airfields, would never be able to launch more than three sorties.

15

Lockheed SR-71: The Quantum Leap

'I WOULD LIKE to announce the successful development of a major new strategic manned aircraft system, which will be deployed by the Strategic Air Command. This system employs the new SR-71 aircraft, and provides a long-range advanced strategic reconnaissance plane for military use, capable of worldwide reconnaissance for military operations...'

With these words, on 25 July 1964, President Lyndon B. Johnson lifted a small corner of the veil that shrouded one of the most secret programmes in the history of military aviation. Johnson went on: 'The SR-71 aircraft will fly at more than three times the speed of sound. It will operate at altitudes in excess of 80,000 feet. It will use the most advanced observation equipment of all kinds in the world. The aircraft will provide the strategic forces of the United States with an outstanding long-range reconnaissance capability. The system will be used during periods of military hostilities and in other situations in which the United States military forces may be confronting foreign military forces...'

The President had got everything right except one point. The aircraft was actually designated RS (Reconnaissance System) 71, but some official decided that it was easier to rename the aircraft than inform Johnson that he had made a mistake.

Work on the SR-71 system began in 1959, when a team led by Clarence L. Johnson, Lockheed's Vice-President for Advanced Development Projects, embarked on the design of a radical new aircraft to supersede the Lockheed U-2 in the strategic reconnaissance role. Designated A-12, the new machine took shape in conditions of the utmost secrecy in the highly restricted section of the Lockheed Burbank plant, the so-called 'Skunk Works', and seven aircraft had been produced by the summer of 1964, when the project's existence was revealed. By that time, the A-12 had already been extensively tested at Edwards AFB, reaching speeds of over 2,000 mph at heights of over 70,000 feet. Early flight tests were aimed at assessing the A-12's suitability as a long-range interceptor, and the experimental interceptor version was shown to the public at Edwards AFB in September 1964, bearing the designation YF-12A.

Two YF-12As were built, equipped with Hughes AN/ASG-18 pulse Doppler fire control radar in a nose radome, infrared sensors and weapon bays in the front section of the fuselage side fairings, which housed an armament of eight Hughes AIM-47A AAMs. On 1 May 1965 the YF-12A set up three world records and six international class records, achieving 2,070.102 mph over a 15/25 km closed circuit, 1,643.042 mph over a 500 km closed circuit, 1,688.891 over a 1,000 km closed circuit with a 2,000 kg payload, and a sustained height of 80,257.91 feet in horizontal flight.

The awesome Lockheed SR-71A Blackbird, unsurpassed by any other manned reconnaissance system.

By this time plans for an operational interceptor version, the F-12B, had fallen victim to changing requirements, defence economies and the downgrading of Air Defense Command in the light of Soviet ICBM developments, but work on the strategic reconnaissance variant went ahead and the prototype SR-71A flew for the first time on 22 December 1964. The first aircraft to be assigned to Strategic Air Command, an SR-71B two-seat trainer (61-7957) was delivered to the 4200th SRW at Beale AFB, California, on 7 January 1966. The 4200th SRW had been activated a year earlier, and by the time the first SR-71 was delivered selected crews had already undergone a comprehensive training programme on Northrop T-38s, eight of which were delivered to Beale from July 1965.

On 25 June 1966, with SR-71 deliveries continuing, the 4200th SRW was redesignated the 9th SRW, its component squadrons becoming the 1st and 99th SRS. This move followed the deactivation of the 9th BW at Mountain Home AFB, and was in keeping with HQ USAF's policy of assuring the continued lineage of units with distinguished records.

The 9th SRW now embarked on a series of intensive operational trials, and in July 1967 the Wing began making supersonic training flights across the United States, having first warned residents in the corridors over which these flights were scheduled to take place that they could expect sonic booms. Because the SR-71 normally operated at about 80,000 feet, the sonic boom it generated resembled distant thunder by the time it reached ground level, and the impact was far less than that produced by, for instance, a low-flying B-58. However, when an SR-71 descended to around 30,000 feet for a refuelling rendezvous with its KC-135 tanker, its sonic boom became more pronounced, particularly during acceleration back to altitude after the completion of refuelling. For this reason, refuelling patterns were established over sparsely populated areas.

A great deal of training time was devoted to familiarisation with the SR-71A's sensory equipment. The main optical sensors included two 48-inch focal length cameras capable of photo-mapping terrain on either side of the aircraft's flight path over a distance of between 833 and 1,619 nautical miles, depending in camera configuration and altitude; the cameras were operated automatically and produced a 1,500-foot strip of black and white, colour or infrared thin base film yielding 1,820 images with a resolution of nine inches. In the nose, an optical bar camera (OBC) was designed to take long-range panoramic oblique photographs over hostile frontiers; the OBC had a focal length of 30 inches and produced a 10,500-foot long, 1,600-frame strip of film with a ground resolution of twelve inches, each frame showing a separate horizon-to-horizon panorama 72 nautical miles wide. With this camera, an SR-71 could photograph a strip of land between 1,478 and 2,930 nautical miles long, again depending on altitude. At its normal operational altitude, and using more than one of its photographic systems, an SR-71 was capable of photographing 60,000 square miles of territory in one hour.

The aircraft also carried a high-resolution side-looking airborne synthetic aperture radar (SLAR) system, able to collect imagery in all weathers, by day or night, of targets between ten and 80 nautical miles on either side of the SR-71 in swathes of ten to 20 miles wide and up to 4,000 nautical miles long. In addition, the SR-71 was fitted with ELINT receivers that could collect electronic data over a 390-nm radius.

With such an advanced system as the SR-71, accidents were inevitable, and three aircraft were lost between April 1967 and January 1968. In each case the crew – pilot and reconnaissance systems operator (RSO) – ejected safely.

Its afterburners streaming flame, a Lockheed SR-71A takes off from RAF Mildenhall. (Colin Lambert)

In the spring of 1968, because of the growing vulnerability of the U-2 in a SAM environment, it was decided to deploy four SR-71s to Kadena air base, Okinawa, for operations over South-East Asia. This deployment, known as *Giant Reach*, was on a 70-day TDY basis, with crews rotating between Beale and Kadena. The aircraft remained in situ and formed the nucleus of Detachment One of the 9th SRW. The first SR-71 mission over Vietnam was flown in April 1968, with up to three missions per week being flown thereafter. Refuelled by a KC-135 on the outward leg, the SR-71 would climb to cruise altitude, and normally penetrate North Vietnamese airspace in the Haiphong area, though this profile depended on operational requirements. The aircraft would then continue over Hanoi, over Laos and into Thailand, where a second air refuelling would take place prior to another reconnaissance run over enemy territory, the aircraft running-in from the Gulf of Tonkin to cover a different area. After a third refuelling over Thailand, the SR-71 would climb out on a direct track back to Kadena. The SR-71's ability to survey an area of 60,000 square miles in one hour meant that it could cover literally hundreds of targets with its long focal length cameras in a single sortie, which would typically last about five and a half hours.

The North Vietnamese made numerous attempts to shoot down the high-flying SR-71s with their SA-2 missiles, but all were confounded by the aircraft's performance and its ECM equipment. No SR-71s were lost to enemy action, although one crashed in Thailand when its engines flamed out in severe turbulence and another was damaged beyond repair when it overran the runway at Kadena. In both cases, the crew escaped unhurt.

During the Paris Peace Talks of 1972 and 1973, flights by Detachment One aircraft over North Vietnam were halted, the SR-71s instead flying stand-off reconnaissance missions over the Gulf of Tonkin. These missions continued after the ceasefire agreement of January 1973. Following the end of hostilities in Vietnam, Detachment One turned its attention to routine surveillance operations off North Korea where border violations by the North had been on the increase. These operations gave rise to allegations that SR-71s had actually penetrated North Korean airspace, but these were strongly denied by the US Government. In fact, the North Koreans claimed that SR-71s infringed their airspace during the first six months of 1981, and on one occasion fired a SAM at an SR-71 that was monitoring North Korean territory from a stand-off position south of the 38th Parallel. The missile detonated several miles away.

In October 1973, following the outbreak of the Yom Kippur War between Egypt and Israel, the 9th SRW was authorised to undertake SR-71 reconnaissance flights over the war zone. Two aircraft were deployed to Griffiss AFB, New York, and on 12 October one of these took off on a direct track for Gibraltar, refuelling twice from KC-135s over the Atlantic. The aircraft then returned to high-speed, high-level cruise to penetrate the Mediterranean, descending again to refuel west of Crete. The SR-71 then carried out a photographic and electronic surveillance of the war zone, covering both northern and southern battlefronts, before returning to Griffiss AFB, again with the aid of flight refuelling, after a total sortie time of just over ten hours and a distance covered of more than 11,000 miles. According to the Egyptians, the SR-71 entered their airspace over Port Said at 11.03 Zulu (GMT), penetrated 366 miles as far as Nagaa Hammady, south of Cairo, turned back over the capital and then flew east towards Jordan and Syria before turning back towards the Mediterranean. The time spent in Egyptian airspace was 25 minutes.

Ten more SR-71 missions were flown over the Middle East between 14 October 1973 and the end of January 1974, some from Griffiss AFB and others from Seymour Johnson AFB, North Carolina. Each flight was of approximately ten hours' duration, including five hours at 3.0M, and involved five flight refuellings. The SR-71's global strategic reconnaissance capability had been proven during a series of trials in 1971, culminating in a record-breaking flight on 26 April that year when a 9th SRW aircraft covered 15,000 miles in ten and a half hours; the concept had now been vindicated under operational conditions.

In 1978–9, SR-71s operating out of Beale AFB flew a brief series of missions over Cuba. Surveillance operations off the island were routine, but on 16 November 1978 the 9th SRW received presidential authority to make an overflight in order to verify that MiG-23 aircraft then being supplied to Cuba were interceptors and not ground attack variants, which were capable of carrying tactical nuclear weapons and whose presence on the island would have violated a pledge given by Moscow in the aftermath of the 1962 missile crisis. The SR-71 flight confirmed that the Russians had not broken their word. Another overflight was made in September 1979 to monitor an apparent buildup of Soviet troops near Havana; it turned out to be a Russian rapid deployment exercise.

SR-71 operations from the United Kingdom began on 20 April 1976, when 64-17972 arrived at RAF Mildenhall on a ten-day TDY. In the years that followed SR-71 deployments to RAF Mildenhall became a regular feature, the UK-based aircraft operating as Detachment Four, 9th SRW. (Detachment Four was originally a U-2 unit, but the U-2s moved to RAF Alconbury in the early 1980s.) Two SR-71s were stationed in the UK at any one time, the aircraft flying stand-off surveillance missions over the Soviet Arctic, the Baltic and the Mediterranean. On 15 and 16 April 1986, two SR-71As of Detachment Four (serial numbers 64-17960 and 64-17980) carried out post-strike reconnaissance following the attacks on Libya (Operation *Eldorado Canyon*) by UK-based F-111s and US Navy aircraft; both SR-71s were used on each occasion.

Post-strike reconnaissance photographs of Benina airfield taken by a Lockheed SR-71A after the American attack on Libya, April 1986.

16

New Technology: The RC-135, U-2R and TR-1

LONG AFTER THE retirement of the RB-47E, the 55th SRW continued to use its mixture of RB-47H/Ks in the ELINT role, its operations being conducted in strict secrecy on a global basis. Unlike the earlier RB-47Es, which had on occasions penetrated Soviet air space, the RB-47H/Ks confined themselves to operations around the periphery of the USSR and its allied countries, for which purpose it maintained permanent detachments in Alaska, the United Kingdom and Japan. The RB-47s were intercepted on numerous occasions by Russian, Chinese and North Korean fighters, and sometimes warning shots were fired, but the RB-47's ability to monitor radio and radar transmissions while standing off in international airspace prevented any serious incidents resulting in the loss of an aircraft.

This record ended abruptly on 1 July 1960, when an RB-47H of the 38th SRS belonging to the 55th SRW's UK-based Detachment One took off from RAF Brize Norton to carry out an ELINT mission over the Barents Sea, with specific reference to Soviet naval facilities on the Kola Peninsula and the nuclear test facility on Novaya Zemlya. The aircraft carried a crew of six. High over the Barents Sea, north of Kola, the RB-47H was intercepted by a MiG-19 fighter of the Soviet 206th Air Division and, according to Russian sources, was signalled to land in Soviet territory. The crew ignored the signals and the Stratojet was shot down. After ten days the Russians announced that they had picked up two survivors; a third crew member, the pilot, was found dead in his life raft. The survivors were prosecuted by the Russians, imprisoned and later repatriated.

The 55th SRW's Detachment Two was located at Yokota AB, Japan, from where its aircraft monitored the Soviet facilities bordering the Sea of Japan, the Sea of Okhotsk, the People's Republic of China and North Korea. Detachment Three was positioned at Eielson AFB, Alaska, and from there the 55th SRW monitored the northeastern sector of the USSR. The RB-47s also tracked Soviet naval movements, their sorties often taking them over the North Pole. Detachment Four operated out of Incirlik, in Turkey, monitoring the southern sector of the USSR and various objectives in the Middle East. This detachment used three specially-modified Stratojets known as EB-47E (TT), with which it monitored Soviet space shots and other missile tests from the launch centres at Baikonur, Tyuratam and Kapustin Yar. This operation was given the code-name *Iron Work* and began late in 1958; one of the aircraft involved was lost in a fatal landing accident in 1962.

By 1966 the 55th SRW was the sole Stratojet operator; it was now reduced to two squadrons, having lost the 338th SRS in 1963 when its strength was reduced to 30

Above, below and opposite: *RC-135s of the 55th SRW pictured at RAF Mildenhall.* (Colin Lambert)

aircraft. In 1966 the other two squadrons moved to Offutt AFB, where in the following year the 55th SRW assumed responsibility for SAC's *Looking Glass* airborne command post operations as well as its normal strategic reconnaissance role, exchanging its Stratojets for RC-135s. The 338th SRS was reactivated briefly during this process to carry on with RB-47 operations while the rest of the wing converted, but it was deactivated again on 25 December. By the end of the year re-equipment with the RC-135 was complete, the last RB-47H (53-4296) having been flown from Offutt AFB to the storage facility at Davis-Monthan AFB on 29 December.

The 55th SRW received 18 RC-135s in all, 14 of them the RC-135V model. Manned by up to 21 linguists and signals specialists from the USAF Electronic Security Command, the RC-135V was a true electronic reconnaissance platform, with an ability to fly twelve-hour sorties using flight refuelling. The surveillance carried out by the RC-135s, under the code name *Rivet Joint*, was (and is) worldwide, the aircraft rotating from Offut AFB to Kadena on Okinawa, Mildenhall in the UK and Hellenikon in Greece, as well as operating from Shemya Island in the Aleutians and Eielson AFB in Alaska. The Kadena-based detachments covered the Kamchatka and Chukotski peninsulas, while those based on Okinawa covered Sakhalin. At the height of the Cold War the Mildenhall-based aircraft flew constant surveillance missions over the Baltic and the Barents Sea, while the RC-135s deployed to Greece covered the southern USSR and the Middle East. Other operations undertaken by the RC-135s have included *Cobra Ball*, which involved monitoring Soviet ICBM tests with two specially-configured RC-135S aircraft carrying equipment to detect telemetry signals from test warheads, and *Combat Sent*, in which two RC-135U aircraft undertook random monitoring operations around the fringes of the Soviet Bloc.

It was during one of the *Cobra Ball* sorties in September 1983, that a Soviet Su-15 fighter destroyed a Korean Air Lines Boeing 747 airliner off Sakhalin Island after it had entered a restricted zone near the Russian naval base at Petropavlovsk. The Russian excuse was that they believed the airliner had been on a spy mission, but the likelihood was that their air defence controllers had confused it with an RC-135 which was in the vicinity. Whatever the truth, the high cold war cost 269 lives that night.

In August 1966, as the 55th SRW awaited re-equipment with the RC-135, the US Defense Department awarded Lockheed a production contract for 13 more U-2s to make good attrition and combat losses suffered by the CIA and USAF in previous years. The CIA, unhappy with the flight characteristics of early-model U-2s, which had grown heavier as more sensory equipment was packed into the airframe, suggested substantial redesign work to correct some of the existing deficiencies and to improve range, payload capability and fatigue life, in the latter case by strengthening the airframe. The cockpit should also be enlarged, the CIA suggested, to improve pilot comfort.

The Lockheed team accordingly began work on modifying the existing U-2A design, which now received the designation U-2R ('R' for Revised) late in 1966. The 17,000-lbst Pratt & Whitney J75-P-13B engine installed in the U-2C was retained, as it was of proven reliability and would provide sufficient power for the new aircraft; fuselage length was increased from 49.7 feet to 62.7 feet, permitting installation of an enlarged cockpit with a 'zero-zero' ejection seat and a bigger Q-bay capable of housing updated sensor systems and ECM equipment; the tail pipe was lengthened to reduce heat emissions; and provision was made for an arrester hook for operations from aircraft carriers. The wingspan was increased from 80.17 feet to 103 feet, the new wing featuring retractable leading edge stall strips, glider-type spoilers to improve control and kill the lift during landing, enlarged fuel tanks and folding wingtips for carrier operations. The wing was also strengthened to permit the mounting of large sensor or fuel pods. The area of the horizontal and vertical tail surfaces was enlarged, and the undercarriage strengthened to compensate for the increase in all-up weight, which went from 24,000 lb to 41,000 lb. Performance was much the same as that of the U-2A series, except that with 1,700 gallons of internal fuel range was increased from 4,700 miles to over 6,200, which greatly increased the aircraft's overseas non-stop deployment capability.

The prototype U-2R flew on 28 August 1967, and the first production U-2Rs were delivered to the CIA at Edwards AFB (North Base) late in 1968. From there, U-2s were deployed to Operating Locations (OLs) in Florida for surveillance of Cuba, and Taiwan for operations over the Chinese mainland. U-2Rs carrying Chinese Nationalist markings and flown by CNAF crews continued to overfly mainland China until 1974, when these operations were halted following a goodwill visit to China by US President Richard Nixon. After that, CIA use of the U-2 gradually declined, until all operations were eventually taken over by the USAF. The latter had, in the meantime, reorganised its strategic reconnaissance assets; in 1966 the 4080th SRW had moved from Laughlin AFB to Davis-Monthan AFB, being re-designated the 100th SRW, and in 1976 another move took the 100th SRW to Beale AFB, where it operated alongside the SR-71As of the 9th SRW. The 9th SRW's U-2 component, the 99th SRS, had been operating in South-East Asia (see Chapter 17), but its various detachments were now brought together at Beale and all remaining USAF U-2 assets were transferred to it, the former U-2 unit designations (4080th and 100th) being allocated to KC-135 tanker units.

In 1969, two U-2Rs were loaned by the CIA to the US Navy for carrier compatibility trials on the USS *America*, the first of a three-day series of deck landing trials being carried out by Lockheed test pilot Bill Park on 21 November. It was found that with a 20-knot wind over the deck, the U-2 could land without having to deploy its arrester hook and that it could also take off with a deck run of 300 feet, without the need of a catapult launch. Following these trials, Lockheed developed a field modification package comprising the arrester hook, wingtip skids, and cockpit arrester hook controls, so that any U-2R could be converted for carrier operations at short notice.

In parallel with this programme, the Navy installed several electronic surveillance systems in the second U-2R, which was designated U-2EP-X. These included an advanced RCA X-band radar and an AN/ALQ-110 Electronic Intelligence Receiver mounted in the Q-bay, and a forward-looking infrared system and forward-looking AN/APS-116 radar mounted in the nose. The systems were to enable the U-2 to patrol vast areas of ocean in the maritime reconnaissance role, the AN/APS-116 being designed to detect submarine periscopes and antennae, and it was proposed to arm some of the U-2s with the Condor anti-ship missile. The programme, however, was discontinued, and the U-2s returned to the CIA.

On 16 November 1979, the U-2R production line was re-opened. The newly-built aircraft were to carry the designation TR-1 (Tactical Reconnaissance 1) in keeping with the aircraft's role, the USAF having decided that stand-off electronic surveillance was now of paramount importance as hostile defence systems became more effective. The new aircraft would be externally similar to the U-2R, although it would incorporate the latest airborne sensor equipment, including the Hughes Advanced Synthetic Aperture Radar System (ASARS) and the Lockheed Precision Emitter Location Strike System (PLSS). ASARS permitted the TR-1, standing-off at high altitude over friendly territory, to undertake cross-border surveillance and tracking of hostile targets, while PLSS was designed to locate hostile radar emitters using the triangulation method, with three TR-1s working together.

Although production of the TR-1 had begun in late 1979, the first flight was actually made in May 1981, by a de-militarised variant, the ER-2 (Earth Resources 2) which was built for NASA. The prototype TR-1A flew on 1 August 1981, closely followed by a second aircraft. After a short flight test programme, the USAF announced that Lockheed had been awarded a production contract for the TR-1; production was to be

A Lockheed TR-1A.

spread over three years, with ten TR-1s being built in 1982, four in 1983 and five in 1984, with a total requirement for 35 aircraft (25 TR-1s and ten U-2R attrition replacement aircraft.) As an interesting aside, it was revealed that some of the U-2Rs were to be allocated to 'meet the needs of non-indigenous intelligence forces', which might be taken to indicate that the RAF was still participating in the U-2 programme, although it might equally imply that the Chinese Nationalists or the Israelis were involved.

The first TR-1A (80-1066) was accepted by SAC on 15 September 1981 and assigned to the 4029th Strategic Reconnaissance Training Squadron of the 9th SRW at Beale AFB. TR-1As and U-2Rs subsequently equipped the 9th SRW's 4025th SRS, 4028th SRS and 99th SRS; a fifth squadron, the 95th SRS, was activated at RAF Alconbury in October 1981 and assumed responsibility for TR-1/U-2R operations from the United Kingdom, coming under the control of the 17th Tactical Reconnaissance Wing.

The 9th SRW subsequently maintained TR-1/U-2R detachments at various OLs around the world. Detachment Two kept one aircraft permanently at Osan air base, South Korea, to monitor events across the 38th Parallel; the Wing rotated one TR-1/ U-2R to RAF Akrotiri, Cyprus, for surveillance of the Middle East and North Africa; and aircraft could be deployed to about 20 OLs worldwide if required. One of these was the island of Diego Garcia, in the Indian Ocean, from where aircraft monitored the Arabian Gulf, Iran and Afghanistan. Quick-reaction deployments were controlled by Detachment 6, based at Norton AFB, California.

TR-1A and U-2R aircraft operating from Patrick AFB in Florida with Detachment 5 of the 9th SRW had Central America as their main area of operations, and among other things they detected a build-up of Soviet arms – including Mi-25 attack helicopters – in Nicaragua during the late 1980s. More recently, both variants were used extensively for surveillance missions during the 1991 Gulf War, and in support of United Nations peacekeeping forces in Bosnia.

17

The Vietnam Experience

THE REQUIREMENT FOR aircraft like the U-2R, with long-range stand-off reconnaissance capability, originated in the Vietnam war, in which United States air power was eventually pitted against a highly sophisticated Russian-supplied air defence system that included the densest concentrations of anti-aircraft weaponry in the history of air warfare.

The American air involvement in Vietnam began in 1961 when President John F. Kennedy approved the establishment of a US combat development and test centre in Vietnam, under the direction of the Defense Department's Advanced Research Projects Agency (DARPA) for the purpose af learning and improving counter-insurgency techniques and tactics. On 14 April 1961, General Curtis E. LeMay, the US Air Force Chief of Staff established the 4400th Combat Crew Training Squadron, code-named *Jungle Jim*, at Eglin AFB, Florida, and on 11 October the President authorised the deployment of a *Jungle Jim* detachment to South Vietnam for training purposes. With the approval of the Saigon government, Detachment 2A of the 4400th Combat Crew Training Squadron, designated *Farm Gate*, became established at Bien Hoa in November–December 1961. It comprised 151 officers and men, eight T-28s, four RC-47s and four RB-26s, all the aircraft bearing South Vietnamese Air Force markings.

The RB-26s, however, were not the first American reconnaissance aircraft to arrive in Vietnam. In the autumn of 1961, Viet Cong guerrilla units operating in considerable strength had begun to cut strategic highways, and USAF advisors in Vietnam asked for the deployment of a detachment of four Republic RF-101 Voodoo tactical reconnaissance aircraft to Tan Son Nhut to carry out reconnaissance missions over Vietnam and Laos. An invitation from the South Vietnamese for the USAF to participate in an air show provided the cover for this deployment, and between 20 October and 21 November 1961 the four RF-101s flew 67 sorties. Early in November, four RF-101s of the Japan-based 45th Tactical Reconnaissance Squadron were deployed to Don Muang Airport in Thailand, firstly to augment and then to replace the detachment at Tan Son Nhut. By the end of 1961, the 45th TRS had flown 130 missions.

In 1962, the South Vietnamese Air Force obtained two camera-equipped Beech C-45s (RC-45s) to conduct photographic reconnaissance flights, but the RF-101 detachment at Don Muang continued to cover the majority of intelligence requirements in Vietnam and Laos. All combat film was processed in Saigon or at an Air Force laboratory at Don Muang, but the time that elapsed between receipt of a request for aerial photographs and their delivery proved much too lengthy in a situation involving fast-moving guerrilla forces operating in jungle terrain. To alleviate the problem, in September 1962 the VNAF, with American support and approval, activated the 716th Reconnaissance Squadron at Tan Son Nhut; equipment comprised the two RC-45s, three RC-47s, 18 RT-28s and several field processing centres. The *Farm Gate* detachment also received an extra pair of RB-26s.

In August 1964, the United States launched its first air strikes against North Vietnam in response to an attack on the destroyer USS *Maddox* by North Vietnamese patrol boats. A second series of air strikes against the North, code-named *Flaming Dart 1*, was launched by the US Navy on 7 February 1965 in retaliation for heavy Viet Cong attacks against US and South Vietnamese military facilities near Pleiku. The next day, USAF aircraft attacked military barracks, photographic coverage being provided by three RF-101s.

By the end of 1965 the USAF was using every reconnaissance system at its disposal to locate enemy targets in the North and to assess bomb damage, including the RB-57 Canberra, the RF-101, and the RF-4C Phantom. (The latter aircraft, equipped with the latest infrared detection gear and SLAR, was deployed to Vietnam late in 1965.) Drones were also used for the first time, the main type being the Ryan 147D; dropped by C-130 Hercules transports, they were used to obtain photographic intelligence of the Hanoi area. Lockheed U-2s had been operating in the theatre since late 1963, when a detachment of the 4080th SRW began overflights of North Vietnam under the code name *Lucky Dragon* (later changed to *Trojan Horse* and finally to *Giant Dragon*), and it was a U-2 which first detected an SA-2 site in North Vietnam on 5 April 1965, intelligence that was confirmed by a low-level photographic mission by a US Navy RF-8A from the USS *Coral Sea*.

In 1965, as the tempo of retaliatory strikes against North Vietnam by the USAF and US Navy increased, the enemy air defences began to deploy growing numbers of radar-

The US experience of SA-2 missiles and other Russian-supplied defences in Vietnam led to the creation of the 'Red Flag' combat training establishment in Nevada. These photographs show a simulated SA-2 Guideline *SAM site.*

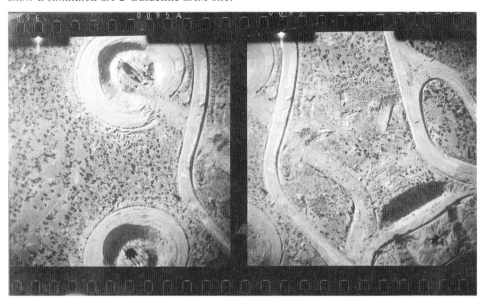

controlled weapon systems, creating a demand for effective ECM. The only source of tactical electronic warfare aircraft readily available was Marine Composite Reconnaissance Squadron One (VMCJ-1) at Iwakuni, Japan, and on 10 April 1965 the Commander-in-Chief, Pacific, ordered the deployment of an electronic warfare detachment to Da Nang. This detachment, under Lieutenant-Colonel Otis W. Corman, was equipped with Douglas EF-10B Skynight aircraft and performed strike support operations until the ageing EF-10Bs were replaced at a later date by the EA-6A, the electronic warfare version of the Grumman A-6 Intruder. In July 1965, six EF-10Bs supported the USAF's first-ever strikes against SAM sites; no attacking aircraft was lost to radar-controlled weapons. In April 1967, following the destruction of a Marine A-4 Skyhawk by an SA-2 missile launched from a site in the Demilitarised Zone (DMZ), EF-10Bs began a continuous patrol along the DMZ during the early hours of darkness, a favourite time for enemy SAM activity. Because of the need for electronic warfare aircraft, the EF-10Bs were not withdrawn from Vietnam until 1969.

The EA-6A made its debut in the Vietnam theatre in November 1966, and at once began electronic warfare support for operations against high-threat areas in the North. With its advanced ECM systems and its ability to follow all manoeuvres carried out by the strike aircraft, the EA-6A represented a quantum leap in the USMC's ECM capability. This capability was further enhanced towards the end of the Vietnam war with the deployment of an even more advanced version, the EA-6B Prowler, which carried two extra ECM specialists.

VMCJ-1's photographic reconnaissance element was equipped with Vought RF-8A Crusaders and, later, McDonnell RF-4B Phantoms. Detachments of RF-8As had been deployed aboard various carriers in the Gulf of Tonkin continually since May 1964, when CinCPac initiated operations code-named *Yankee Team* to conduct photo

The camera's eye view of a simulated Russian fighter airfield, taken on a Nato 'Red Flag' exercise in Nevada.

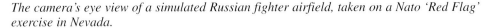

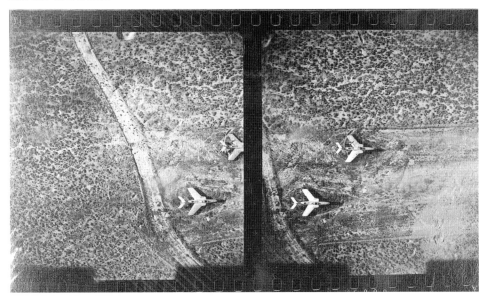

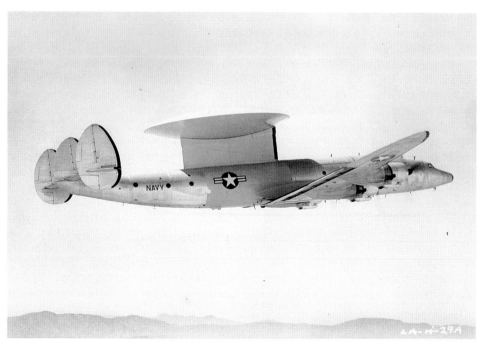

A Lockheed WV-2.

reconnaissance over Laos. Detachment pilots also provided post-strike reconnaissance in conjunction with the Navy's first air strikes against North Vietnam, and continued PR activities as part of carrier air wings until rejoining their parent unit at Da Nang in December 1965. With the RF-8A, photographic coverage of large areas in search of firm intelligence of enemy movements was confined to daylight hours and periods of good weather. Replacement of the RF-8A with the multi-sensor RF-4B, beginning in October 1966, provided VMCJ-1 with a round-the-clock intelligence-gathering capability, and as experience was gained with the new systems, night infra-red reconnaisance played an increasing part in the overall intelligence collection effort.

By the end of 1965 USAF and USN reconnaissance aircraft had pinpointed 56 SA-2 sites in North Vietnam, but as American pilots were forced to lower attack altitudes in order to avoid the SAMs it was conventional AAA and small-arms automatic fire that accounted for most of the combat losses. In fact, of the 180 or so SA-2s launched in 1965, only eleven succeeded in destroying an aircraft. Nevertheless, an electronic war developed as the Americans strove to counter the enemy's network of radar controlled guns, SAMs and defensive radars; the role of the USMC's EF-10Bs in this battle has already been mentioned, but the USAF made increasing use of the Douglas EB-66, an electronic warfare version of the RB-66C tactical reconnaissance aircraft, whose equipment detected emissions from the SA-2's *Fan Song* tracking radar and employed countermeasures against it. (The RB-66C, which replaced the RB-57A Canberra, equipped the 363rd Tactical Reconnaissance Wing in the USA and the 10th TRW in Europe; one of the latter's aircraft was lost on an operational sortie over East Germany on 10 March 1964.)

As a countermeasure against North Vietnamese interceptors, the USAF deployed several EC-121 early warning aircraft to Da Nang early in 1965. The history of this aircraft went back to 1950–51, when the US Navy acquired two Lockheed Model 749 Constellations and, under the designation WV-1, modified them to test advanced electronic surveillance systems. The trials proved satisfactory, and the US Navy ordered into production a version of the Model 1049 Super Constellation to serve as a high altitude reconnaissance and early warning radar intelligence aircraft, designated WV-2. Powered by four 3,350 hp Wright Turbo Compound engines, the WV-2 carried some $5\frac{1}{2}$ tons of electronic equipment, including a General Electric height-finding radar in a 7-ft high upper fuselage radome, and surveillance radar in a large radome under the fuselage. The fuselage interior housed a complete Combat Information Centre for co-ordination and transmission of intelligence data, and five radar consoles/plotting stations permitted full analysis of incoming data. The WV-2 normally carried a 30-strong double crew on long range early warning missions, or one crew of 19 on shorter electronic reconnaissance sorties. The WV-2E was an improved variant with a very large radar scanner in a lenticular housing mounted on a pylon above the fuselage, while the WV-3 was a weather reconnaissance variant. The first delivery of a WV-2 took place in July 1952 to Early Warning Squadron VW-2.

The EC-121C and EC-121D were variants of the WV-2 for the USAF, and in fact the USN's WV-2s were re-designated EC-121 in the early 1960s. Between 1955 and 1965, the US Navy's WV-2s/EC-121s were responsible for early warning coverage of the North Atlantic, this being taken over by ground radar stations in August 1965. The last AEW patrol in this connection was flown by an EC-121J Warning Star of VW-11 (Keflavik, Iceland) on 26 August 1965. In USAF service, EC-121s equipped the 551st and 552nd AEW and Countermeasures Wings of Air Defense Command, one covering the Atlantic seaboard of the USA and the other the Pacific. On 14 April 1969, a US Navy EC-121 became the last major military casualty of the high cold war when it was shot down by North Korean fighters while carrying out a routine surveillance mission from Atsugi, Japan, over the Sea of Japan; all 31 crew members perished.

Operating off the coast of North Vietnam, the 'Big Look' EC-121s were not only able to alert US aircraft of approaching MiGs and SAM launches, but also served as airborne radar and communications platforms. In addition, they warned American pilots who flew too near the Chinese border and assisted air-sea rescue searches for ditched aircrew. Later, the EC-121's equipment was integrated with the US Navy's ship-based radars, enabling US pilots to obtain a variety of timely additional information about the enemy's and their own air operations over the North. In 1966, during the US *Rolling Thunder* bombing campaign against the North, the EC-121s were of great help in alerting F-4 Phantom crews operating at low level to the presence of missile-armed MiGs, enabling them to spot the more manoeuvrable fighters in good time and to use their higher acceleration and speed in hit and run tactics. During the first phase of *Rolling Thunder*, EC-121s, supported by US Navy EA-3Bs, issued 141 SAM warnings and 38 MiG warnings.

The US Navy's EC-121s and EA-3Bs were operated by Electronic Warfare Squadrons VQ-1 and VQ-2, the EA-3Bs being deployed on board aircraft carriers. The EA-3B was the electronic warfare version of the Douglas A-3 Skywarrior (the B-66 being the USAF variant of this aircraft) and the RA-3 equipped the Navy's heavy photographic squadrons, whose primary mission was to supply the Navy with cartographic photography. In Vietnam, RA-3Bs, equipped with infrared sensors and video real time displays, were used to locate Viet Cong movements at night and call in

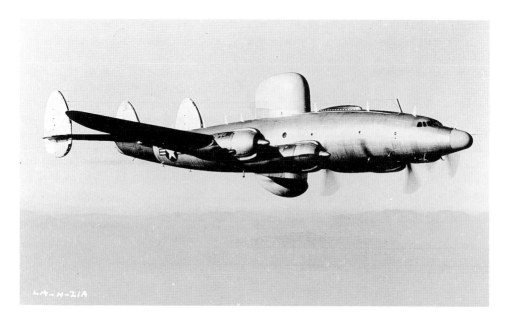

The Lockheed EC-121 provided invaluable service in Vietnam.

strike aircraft. During the bombing pause of 1968, RA-3Bs of VAP-61 flew intelligence-gathering missions over the Ho Chi Minh Trail, and operations in Vietnam were also supported by detachments from VAP-62, which normally served with the Atlantic Fleet.

The US Navy's tactical photo-reconnaissance aircraft at the start of the Vietnam war was the RF-8A Crusader, and in 1965 Fleet photographic fighter units began converting to the updated RF-8G, which had provision for underwing pylons, new cameras, sensors, electronics and a new navigation system. RF-8Gs were deployed on Essex-class carriers, normally in detachments of three aircraft provided by Light Photographic Squadrons VFP-62 or VFP-63.

The Navy's real photo-reconnaissance workhorse throughout operations in Vietnam, however, was the North American RA-5C Vigilante, the PR version of the A-5 supersonic attack bomber. The majority of A-5A and A-5B airframes were converted to RA-5C configuration, and as the RA-5C replaced the attack variant in US Navy service the squadrons equipped with the Vigilante were redesignated as RVAH (Reconnaissance Heavy Attack) squadrons. First service deliveries of the RA-5C were made in January 1964 to VAH-3, the training squadron for Heavy Attack Wing One, and Reconnaissance Attack Squadron 5 (RVAH-5) became operational on the USS *Ranger* in the South China Sea in June that year, the first of ten RA-5C squadrons to be activated; of these, eight were to see service in Vietnam, originally deployed in units of six aircraft. This was later reduced to three as combat losses and normal attrition took their toll.

The RA-5C could be fitted with a variety of sensors, including radar, infra-red, TV

The North American RA-5C Vigilante, reconnaissance workhorse of the Vietnam War. Note the under-fuselage 'canoe' type recce pod.

and electromagnetic, and strobe lights could be carried under the wings for night photography. The reconnaissance systems were housed in a long 'canoe' fairing under the fuselage, and extra fuel cells were installed in the linear bomb bay. The Vigilante's surveillance systems were directly linked to a new integrated operational intelligence centre (IOIC) in the parent carrier; the IOIC gathered all the photographic and electronic information collected by the aircraft and disseminated it to the fleet.

The RA-5C proved so successful in action over Vietnam that the production line was reopened in 1969 and an additional 48 aircraft built. Eighteen aircraft were lost on operations.

As mentioned in Chapter 15, Strategic Air Command deployed SR-71A reconnaissance aircraft to South-East Asia in 1968 for operations over Vietnam. Also in 1968, the USAF U-2 detachment at OL-20, Bien Hoa, was brought up to squadron strength and designated 99th SRS. In July 1970 the unit was transferred to U-Tapao in Thailand, from where it flew pre- and post-strike reconnaissance missions (code-named *Olympic Torch*) in support of Operation *Linebacker II*, the renewed air offensive against North Vietnam. During this period the 99th SRS also monitored Chinese communications (Operation *Senior Book*). The squadron remained in Thailand until December 1974, its aircraft and crews then being dispersed to other U-2 detachments at OLs in various parts of the world.

Linebacker II, which was authorised by President Nixon in May 1972 against the background of a major North Vietnamese Army offensive against the south and a stalemate at the Paris peace talks, is worth examining in some detail, because it brought together all the photographic intelligence and electronic intelligence resources, as well as all the ECM facilities, employed so far in Vietnam. As part of the renewed offensive, B-52s ventured into heavily defended North Vietnamese air space for the first time in May and June to make limited night attacks on airfields and oil storage facilities, and also to lay mines in the waters of Haiphong and other strategic ports. These minelaying operations, carried out by modified B-52Ds, were also flown under cover of darkness, and no losses were sustained.

On 20 October 1972, when it seemed as though the Paris talks were at last leading to an agreement that would end the war, air operations over North Vietnam were once more halted. They were resumed when the peace talks again broke down amid indications that the North Vietnamese were preparing to renew their offensive in the South. There followed an eleven-day bombing campaign against the North which developed into the heaviest bombing offensive of the war, with round-the-clock attacks on targets which had mostly been on the restricted list until then. They included rail yards, power plants, communications facilities, POL stores and ammunition supply dumps, as well as the principal NVAF fighter bases and SAM sites. The target list numbered 34 strategic objectives, over 60 per cent of which were situated within a 25-mile radius of Hanoi.

The original plan called for the B-52s to attack at night, in three waves, with F-111s and A-6s continuing the offensive in daylight. The B-52 bomber streams were to be preceded by F-111 interdictors, attacking fighter bases at low level, and F-4 Phantoms dropping *Window*. The B-52s were to approach their target areas from the north-west, using strong high-altitude winds to give them a much increased ground speed, and after bomb release they were to swing away from the target in tight turns in order to clear SAM defences as quickly as possible. Attacks would be made by cells of three aircraft, generally bombing from 33,000 feet. The three aircraft were to fly in close formation

A Boeing B-52D on Guam, being armed for a mission against North Vietnam.

to pool their ECM resources, which included the GE ALQ-87 and ITT ALQ-117 jammers and the Lundy ALE-24 chaff dispensing system. In fact, the B-52D was better equipped with ECM than SAC's main force B-52Gs, some of which were brought in to augment the bombing force during *Linebacker II*.

The operation began on the night of 18/19 December 1972, when 129 B-52s took off from their respective bases in Thailand and on Guam. Thirty minutes before the first cells arrived over their targets, F-111s carried out strikes on enemy airfields and F-4s sowed two chaff corridors to screen the attacks on the target areas of Kinh No and Yen Vien, north of Hanoi. Unfortunately, the strong north-west wind had dispersed the chaff before the B-52s arrived.

The first B-52 wave to attack the Yen Vien rail yards flew over a cluster of SAM sites as it began its final run-in to the target, and *Charcoal 1* – the leading aircraft in the 'Charcoal' cell – sustained a near miss from an SA-2 just as its bomb doors were opening. Crippled and out of control, with its pilot, co-pilot and gunner either dead or incapacitated, the bomber began its long plunge to earth. The navigator, radar navigator and electronic warfare officer ejected and were taken prisoners. A second B-52, attacking with 'Peach' cell in the second wave four hours later, was luckier; it was also crippled by an SA-2, this time just after completing its bombing run, but managed to reach friendly territory with wing and engine fires before its crew were forced to abandon it.

The third wave of 18 B-52s, attacking five hours later, encountered fierce opposition over the target (the Hanoi railway repair shops). More than 60 SAM launches were observed, but the bombers' ECM worked well and there were no losses, although one aircraft was damaged by a near miss. Another wave of 21 aircraft, attacking from the west, also encountered heavy opposition from eleven SAM sites in the Hanoi area and lost the leading aircraft in the last cell to bomb, *Rose 1*. On this first night of *Linebacker II*, therefore, in which the enemy had launched more than 200 SAMs and expended massive quantities of AAA ammunition, the SA-2s had destroyed three B-52s and damaged three more. Enemy fighters had also been airborne, and a MiG-21 was shot down in a radar-directed gun engagement by Staff Sergeant Samuel O. Turner, the tail gunner in a B-52D. A second MiG was also to fall to the B-52s' gunners before the eleven-day campaign was over.

The B-52s suffered no casualties on the night of 19/20 December, when 120 bombers attacked several targets in the Hanoi area. However, the North Vietnamese had by now realised that the bombers were approaching their target areas along the same tracks each night, and they evolved new tactics that included sending up MiGs to shadow the incoming bomber stream and verify its altitude, so that the defences could fuze their missile warheads and AAA shells accordingly.

During the third night of operations, on 20/21 December, SA-2s knocked down two B-52s as they completed their bombing runs, and both of them crashed in Hanoi. ('You can't imagine', said one Phantom pilot who was in the vicinity and who saw the bombers go down, 'how it sends shivers up and down your spine to watch a B-52 come down from 30,000 feet. It takes a long time to hit the ground...') A third B-52, badly damaged, struggled back to Thailand, only to crash on landing, killing four of its crew. Two more B-52s in the last wave that night were destroyed by SAMs; a third was crippled and crashed in Laos. In the nine-hour operation the enemy had fired 220 SAMs and claimed six B-52s, four of which were B-52Gs.

On the fourth night, 21/22 December, the tactics employed by the bomber stream were modified. The time between attacking waves was greatly reduced, attacking altitudes were varied and the cells were randomly spaced. In addition, individual crews were given freedom of action in evasive manoeuvring; most favoured a shallow post-attack turn followed by a dive to low altitude and a high-speed run clear of the Vietnamese defences over the Gulf of Tonkin. All sorties on this night were flown from U-Tapao, the Guam-based B-52s being released for *Arc Light* missions (carpet-bombing attacks on suspected NVA troop movements in the South) and there were no losses.

The B-52 force was stood down for 36 hours over the Christmas period, but on the night of 26/27 December 120 B-52s, flying in tightly compressed waves and accompanied by 113 defence suppression and ECM aircraft, attacked ten targets in Hanoi, Haiphong and Thai Nguyen, the more vulnerable B-52Gs being assigned to the latter objectives. Two streams attacked Hanoi from the north-west, flying in from Laos and out over the Gulf of Tonkin, while two more attacked on a reciprocal track. All the bombers passed through the target areas within 15 minutes and only one B-52 fell to the SAM defences, although a second, severely damaged, crashed short of the runway while attempting to land at U-Tapao.

The last three nights of *Linebacker II*, in which 60 B-52s were committed on each night, cost SAC five more bombers, all victims of SAMs. By this time the North Vietnamese defences had been virtually neutralised, and the enemy had expended most of their stock of about 1,000 SA-2s. On 30 December, North Vietnam announced that it was ready to resume peace negotiations.

In all, 729 B-52 sorties had been flown during *Linebacker II*, and more than 15,000 tons of bombs dropped out of a total of 20,370 tons. Fifteen B-52s had been lost to the SAM defences, and nine damaged. Thirty-four targets had been hit, and some 1,500 civilians killed. Of the 92 crew members aboard the shot-down bombers, 26 were recovered by rescue teams, 29 were listed as missing, and 33 baled out over North Korea to be taken prisoner and later repatriated.

Many lessons were learned in Vietnam that would be applied to future airborne intelligence gathering systems. Foremost among them was that for a manned reconnaissance aircraft to survive in a hostile high-technology air defence environment, it literally had to be invisible to radar and other electronic sensors as it carried out its mission. Research that would lead to the production of an operational 'stealth' aircraft was already more than a decade old when the Vietnam War ended, but it was that unhappy conflict that accelerated the programme and made the Lockheed F-117A strike/reconnaissance aircraft and the Northrop B-2 bomber a reality.

Meanwhile, the strategic reconnaissance 'war' had taken a new twist. While the Vietnam War was being fought, the Soviet Union, in the space of a few short years, had assumed the proportions of a major maritime power, armed with a formidable capability to disrupt the vital ocean links between Europe and North America and to visit unthinkable destruction on the NATO alliance. Constant maritime surveillance of the Soviet Navy's movements was now a matter of the utmost priority.

18

Russian Reconnaissance: The Bid for Maritime Supremacy

WHEN THE GERMANS launched their invasion of the Soviet Union in June 1941, they did so with the advantage of almost complete surprise, and were consequently able to inflict appalling losses on the Russians during the early weeks of the campaign. If the Russians had possessed strategic reconnaissance aircraft, that element of surprise might have been stripped away; but they did not, and even as the war progressed the Soviet Air Force leadership, while producing battlefield reconnaissance and observation aircraft in considerable numbers, continued to neglect the strategic aspect.

At the war's end the two principal Soviet long-range reconnaissance aircaft were the Petlyakov Pe-2R and the Tupolev Tu-2R, both modifications of existing light bomber designs. They were equipped with three cameras for vertical and oblique photography and the Tu-2R had an extended wingspan to improve its altitude performance. Both continued to serve in the reconnaissance role until they were replaced by the Ilyushin Il-28R, the reconnaissance version of the twin-jet bomber, around 1950; but this was still essentially a tactical aircraft, with a speed and altitude performance inferior to its rough equivalent, the Canberra, and so were the aircraft that replaced it in turn, the Yak-25R and Yak-28R.

The only real attempt by the Russians to produce a high-altitude strategic reconnaissance aircraft in the 1950s resulted in the Yak-RV, a development of the well-proven Yak-25 with 70-ft high aspect ratio wings fitted with tip tanks. On 13 July, 1959, a Major Smirnov reached an altitude of over 67,000 feet in this aircraft while carrying a 2,200-lb payload, and operational deployment of the Yak-RV is thought to have begun in 1963. Very little is known about the aircraft, of which only a few examples are believed to have been built, but in the 1960s there were reports that it had made incursions into Indian air space. Its main use, following the deterioration of Sino–Soviet relations, was probably to maintain surveillance of Chinese territory, particularly after the Chinese detonated their first nuclear device in 1964. The aircraft was given the NATO reporting name *Mandrake*. At a later date the Russians produced a reconnaissance version of the MiG-25 *Foxbat* interceptor, the MiG-25R, which was equipped with cameras and side-looking radar, and in the early 1980s Myasishchev built an approximate U-2 equivalent, the M-17 *Mystic*, with a high aspect ratio wing and a twin-boom tail. Powered by a single jet engine, the M-17 could reach heights of over 70,000 feet.

The point about the Soviet intelligence-gathering system was that it was never subjected to the same constraints, restrictions and blind spots as the West's. The western world was positively crawling with intelligence sources, from military publications to the Soviet agents and sympathisers who by the mid-1950s had infiltrated every western intelligence agency at senior levels. The Russians had no need of overflights to locate potential targets; the information they needed was readily available to them. For electronic and signals intelligence gathering they made considerable use of modified deep-sea trawlers (AGIs), which made close approaches to NATO coastlines to monitor radar transmissions and communications. One of the first aircraft modified for ELINT/SIGINT work was the twin-jet Tupolev Tu-14 bomber (NATO reporting name *Bosun*) operated by some units of the Soviet Naval Air Arm; other aircraft subsequently modified were the Antonov An-12 *Cub* and Ilyushin Il-18 *Coot*, the Beriev Be-6 *Madge* flying boat and its turboprop-powered successor, the Be-12 *Mail*.

In the 1950s, new Soviet defence policies led to a major expansion of strategic air reconnaissance capabilities, with the emphasis on maritime surveillance. From the late 1940s to the late 1950s, the main Russian naval concern was defence of the coastal areas of the Soviet Union; more than 50 per cent of Russian submarines and more than 70 per cent of surface ships and patrol craft were designed for this purpose. By 1958, Soviet naval forces comprised nearly 900 surface vessels and 550 diesel-powered submarines, about 250 of which (the Whiskey and Zulu classes) were capable of conducting combat operations on the open seas. The first four Whiskey class attack boats transited from the Baltic to Ulone Bay, Albania, in August 1958. Prior to this, the sight of Soviet warships of any type on the high seas was extremely rare, except for occasional transfers of units between the Baltic and Northern Fleets. These transfers were always carried out in great haste and gave an impression that the Russians felt somewhat uncomfortable outside the waters of their own fleet areas.

In 1958 a new phase of development commenced when programmes initiated in the 1953–54 period began to reach fruition. The clear objective now was to extend the maritime defensive perimeter around the USSR, primarily to counter the threat posed to Soviet territory by nuclear-capable US carrier aircraft, but also to extend the operational radius of new submarines and surface vessels capable of delivering ballistic or cruise missiles. On 29 May 1959, for the first time, NATO maritime forces tracked a submerged Zulu class submarine converted to carry ballistic missiles in the Norwegian Sea.

By the beginning of 1960, routine surveillance by US and British ELINT and PR aircraft had revealed much new construction work in progress at the Soviet Northern Fleet's main operational bases on the Murmansk area, while there was a steady buildup of strategic aircraft on the principal airfields, mainly Severomorsk. The growing sensitivity of the area was underlined when, on 1 July 1960, an RB-47H Stratojet of the 55th SRW from RAF Brize Norton was shot down over the Barents Sea, north of the Kola Peninsula, by a MiG-19 interceptor flown by Lt Vasili Poliakov. Two of the RB-47's crew of six survived, were picked up and subsequently repatriated after seven months in Russian captivity.

The first clear indication that the Russians were adopting an increasingly bold fleet policy, with the deployment of new and modern warships supported by attack and ELINT aircraft, came in 1961. In July of that year the first significant Soviet out-of-area exercise took place, with eight surface combatant units, associated support vessels

A Myasishchev Mya-4 Bison *pictured on an ELINT operation over the North Atlantic.*

and four submarines exercising in the Norwegian Sea. This was followed, in 1962, by the first transfer between the Black Sea and Northern Fleets, and an exercise in July included four surface units plus support ships and more than 20 submarines, operating within an exercise area that extended from the Iceland–Faeroes Gap to North Cape. Soviet maritime aircraft also took part in strength, and reconnaissance variants of the three Russian strategic bombers then in service, the Tu-16 *Badger*, Tu-95 *Bear* and Mya-4 *Bison*, were all identified and seen to be equipped for flight refuelling.

The Cuban crisis of October 1962 taught the Russians a stern lesson in the importance of sea power, and future Soviet naval policies were amended accordingly. A pattern of bi-annual exercises was established in 1963. In March and April seven surface units plus support ships exercised near the Lofotens, and in August a similar force conducted exercises in the Iceland–Faeroes Gap. Part of this group circumnavigated the British Isles before returning to the Baltic. Inter-fleet transfers between Northern, Baltic and Black Sea Fleets continued and intensified. The exercises of 1964 saw the introduction of the latest missile-carrying warships; fleet strengths were increased and the scope and type of exercises in areas between North Cape and the Faeroes Gap revealed more imagination and expertise. The Soviet Mediterranean Squadron (the 5th *Eskadra*) was also established on a continuing basis – although small numbers of submarines had been in the Mediterranean since 1958 – and there was a transfer of ships to Cuba. Tu-95 *Bear* ELINT aircraft were leaving their bases in north Russia and flying non-stop to Cuba, often in pairs, gathering intelligence

Opposite: *Tupolev Tu-95* Bear *ELINT aircraft over the Norwegian Sea.*

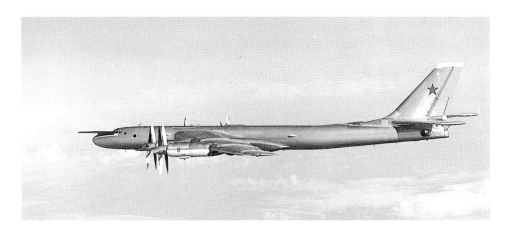

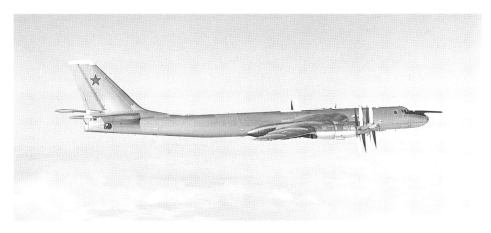

on NATO fleet movements in the Atlantic en route, then repeating the process in reverse a week or so later.

The spring work-up of 1965 involved only a small force near the North Cape. In the summer, however, a full-scale manoeuvre ranging from the Iceland approaches through the Iceland–Faeroes Gap to North Cape took place, involving about 30 combatant units plus support ships and a large number of submarines. In the Mediterranean, the Soviet Squadron increased its presence but remained in the eastern half with little activity. In 1966, referring to the growth and presence of Soviet sea power during 1965, Admiral V. A. Kasatonov, First Deputy C-in-C of the Soviet Navy, commented, 'The USSR Navy flag can be seen in all parts of the world's oceans. The aim of these excursions is to support the national interests of the Soviet Union. At present, our ships are undergoing naval training in parts of the world's oceans which earlier used to be the traditional preserve of the British and American navies.'

Activity in 1966 consisted mainly of patrol and surveillance duties in the North Sea, off the Shetland Islands and in the Norwegian Sea. Again there was an exercise near North Cape, and for the first time the basic work-up exercise was conducted in the Iceland–Faeroes Gap. Meanwhile, the Mediterranean Squadron continued a slow build-up.

The May exercise of 1967 involved a large number of surface units and submarines operating in the Norwegian Sea, with isolated ASW exercises taking place in the Iceland–Faeroes Gap and off North Cape. The dramatic event of 1967 was the Arab–Israeli Six-Day War; Soviet reaction included port visits to Syria, Egypt, Yugoslavia and Algeria, with increased ELINT operations over the eastern Mediterranean. These were carried out mainly by *Badgers*, although *Mails* were occasionally identified. At the same time unit deployments were increased and lengthened, with Soviet warships venturing as far south as the Canary Islands and passing through the English Channel en route to and from the Mediterranean.

In 1968, a small exercise in the Iceland–Faeroes Gap in May and surveillance of a NATO exercise off the Lofoten Islands prefaced the largest Soviet out-of-area exercise ever held. Exercise *Sever* (North), which was held in the Norwegian Sea, was a multi-phased, multi-areas operation involving a very large number of surface units, submarines and aircraft. Later, from October to December, a small force patrolled an area off north-east Scotland and a single vessel patrolled north of the Faeroes in August. In the Mediterranean, force levels were maintained and deployments lengthened. A new ASW helicopter carrier, the *Moskva*, entered the Mediterranean for the first time in September.

The spring exercise of 1969 began in the Iceland–Faeroes Gap during March and involved a large number of ships. During this period, the first large-scale relief of Mediterranean forces by the Northern Fleet took place, and an ASW exercise was conducted in the Norwegian Sea. Other exercises took place in the North Sea and the area of Jan Mayen Island.

On 14 April 1970 the Soviet Ministry of Defence announced that a naval exercise, named *Okean*, was to be conducted in the Atlantic and Pacific Oceans. The exercise started rather badly when a Soviet nuclear submarine sank in the Atlantic on 12 April. That same week a Soviet replenishment auxiliary convoy of nine ships appeared north of North Cape and proceeded to an exercise area at approximately 72°N 02°E; it was followed two days later by two surface task groups from the Northern Fleet, bringing the total deployed strength to 26 ships. Anti-submarine warfare exercises were conducted west of the Lofoten Islands from 13 to 18 April, and on 21 April an exercise with forces from the Mediterranean and the Northern Fleet Battle Group was scheduled in an area centred on approximately 57°N 20°W in the Atlantic, with replenishment of the two major groups taking place between the Faeroes and Shetlands. Two groups of surface vessels also moved out of the Baltic and operated off southwest Norway, while a landing exercise was held off North Cape.

During the decade of Soviet naval expansion, western intelligence analysts were able to identify all the reconnaissance and ELINT versions of Russia's trio of strategic bombers and assess their roles. The first variant of the Tu-95 to be used for maritime surveillance was the *Bear B*, but it was the *Bear D* which was the first to be equipped fully for electronic warfare, reconnaissance and targeting. In August 1967 one of these aircraft was extensively photographed by US icebreakers in the Kara Sea (a long way from home, and suspiciously close to the USSR's Novaya Zemlya nuclear test site) as it made several runs overhead. It had a large number of modifications, including a large ventral radome for X-band radar, and was clearly designed to operate in conjunction with Soviet nuclear submarines and surface vessels, gathering visual and electronic intelligence and providing long-range target data for missile crews.

The version of the Tu-16 used for electronic intelligence was the *Badger F*, joined in 1969 or thereabouts by a maritime reconnaissance version of the supersonic Tupolev Tu-22 jet bomber, the *Blinder C*. As well as being equipped for ELINT and ECM, this aircraft also carried a battery of six cameras for the PR role. The *Blinder C* was sighted in June 1971, when the Soviet Northern Fleet conducted an exercise that followed the traditional 'defence of the homeland' theme evident in *Okean 70*. However, in a significant departure from former practice in the Norwegian Sea, the Soviet forces conducted extensive anti-submarine warfare operations in an area north-east of Jan Mayen Island. Additionally, an exercise apparently aimed at establishing a defence against a carrier task force was conducted further south, around 70°N, while an amphibious exercise was carried out in local waters north of the Kola peninsula.

There were no major Soviet naval exercises in 1972; instead, the Russians used the NATO naval exercise *Strong Express* to sharpen their surveillance and targeting procedures, with *Badger* and *Bear* reconnaissance aircraft very much in evidence. April 1973 saw exercise *Springex 73*, with activities concentrated in the Norwegian Sea and the Iceland–UK Gap; the theme was mainly anti-submarine warfare, and surface units, submarines and ASW aircraft took part in the operations. Heavy concentrations of submarines in the well-defined choke points of the exercise area were detected. These submarines, if allowed to take up similar positions in time of conflict, would present a considerable threat to any NATO attempt to reinforce the northern flank.

Springex 74, conducted in late May, was held over a considerably shorter time frame than previous Soviet exercises witnessed in the Norwegian Sea, but was no less significant than its predecessors. Although no obvious scenario presented itself, air, surface and subsurface units operated in two main areas between Jan Mayen Island and Iceland and between Iceland and the UK. The theme of the exercise seemed to be one of surveillance and quick reaction, and this pattern of activity was again repeated during the NATO exercises *Quick Shave* and *Swift Move* conducted later in the year. The Russians used both these NATO exercises to enhance their own monitoring and surveillance capabilities.

In April 1975, everything the Russians had learned so far appeared to come together

Caught in the act: a Bear *is shadowed by a USAF Phantom off Alasaka.*

Soviet electronic intelligence gathering was carried out by the Ilyushin Il-38 May, *the military version of the Il-18 civil airliner, in addition to maritime patrol.*

An Il-38 May *caught in the act of deploying a sonobuoy.*

in the largest maritime exercise ever witnessed. Over 200 ships and submarines and large numbers of aircraft participated in a centrally co-ordinated worldwide operation. The exercise areas included the Norwegian Sea, the North and Central Atlantic, the Baltic and Mediterranean Seas and the Indian and Pacific Oceans. Submarine activity in the Atlantic was concentrated in the gap between Iceland and Jan Mayen Island and off the west coast of Ireland. All phases and methods of modern naval warfare were practised, including the deployment of strategic nuclear submarines. The exercise was also significant in that it included the participation of merchant shipping in a convoy role, and a simulated convoy off North Cape was the subject of intensive air attacks. Soviet aircraft were also observed operating with surface units north of the Azores. In addition to ELINT aircraft, Tu-126 AWACS (Airborne Warning and Control System) aircraft also took part. Known to NATO as *Moss*, the Tu-126 was a military version of the Tu-114 civil airliner and was fitted with a 36-ft lenticular radar scanner above the fuselage.

In late June 1976 the Russians conducted an exercise which began in the North Sea and continued into the Baltic, but the maritime event of the year was the emergence of the Soviet capital ship *Kiev* from the Black Sea in July. This ship, designated by NATO as a missile-equipped anti-submarine warfare carrier, deployed into the Atlantic after a moderate amount of exercise and training in the Mediterranean. While in the Mediterranean, the Russians took the opportunity to demonstrate their new Yak-38 *Forger* V/STOL strike aircraft, as well as Kamov Ka-25 *Hormone* ASW helicopters. The *Kiev* entered the Soviet Northern Fleet area early in August.

In 1977, the Soviet exercise *Springex I* began during mid-April, with activities concentrated on anti-submarine warfare operations conducted north of North Cape and

The Russian carrier Kiev *under surveillance by an RAF Nimrod maritime reconnaissance aircraft.*

in the central Norwegian Sea. The exercise included air, surface and subsurface units which carried out operations on a broader scale, although with less co-ordination between the surface attack groups than in previous years. Subsequently, *Springex II* was conducted in mid-June in the Atlantic and Barents Sea, with 27 surface units and 160 aircraft carrying out an air-to-surface strike exercise.

The Soviet exercise *Springex 78* was conducted in mid-April in association with the transit of a Kiev class vessel, the *Minsk*, from the Mediterranean to the Northern Fleet. The most interesting aspect of this exercise was the area in which the Russians began operations, a locale which had never been used before in an exercise. The area was south of the Iceland–Faeroes Gap, in proximity to major NATO bases. On the whole, the exercise was brief and greatly reduced in composition compared with previous years, although demonstrating a certain flexibility and vigour in execution. In the following year, *Springex 79* was conducted in two phases, the first involving the transfer of a Kiev class vessel from the Mediterranean to the Northern Fleet, and all participants conducted anti-carrier warfare operations. The exercise included 25 surface ships, eleven submarines and 250 aircraft sorties, the first reconnaissance flight (by a *Bear*) being conducted west-south-west of the British Isles. The theme of the second phase was anti-submarine warfare; it involved all units that had participated in phase one and was conducted from the vicinity of Rockall to the North Cape.

The Russians did most of their intelligence gathering by means of specially converted trawlers (AGIs) like this one, caught off northern Scotland by a Nimrod.

In April 1980, a Soviet naval exercise was carried out as a Kiev class ship left the Mediterranean en route for the Northern Fleet. Three Krivak class frigates departed the Baltic and joined the Kiev group west of Land's End. The units conducted anti-submarine warfare operations west of Ireland with three submarines located in the area. ELINT and ASW aircraft operated south-west over the Norwegian Sea, through the Greenland–UK Gap to an area west of Rockall. The Krivaks entered the Mediterranean and the Kiev group continued north and carried out two days of simulated air to surface strikes while sailing to join the Northern Fleet.

A Soviet Northern Fleet exercise was conducted early in July 1981, activities being concentrated north-west of North Cape and east of 30 degrees. The theme was mainly anti-submarine warfare conducted with surface ships, submarines and ASW aircraft. The surface units formed three different groups (two groups from the Northern Fleet and one joining the Northern Fleet from the Baltic). A heavier concentration of aircraft throughout the whole exercise formed a major difference from previous years, when aircraft tended to be active for only one or two days.

There were no major Soviet naval exercises in 1982, but there was nevertheless a significant development, and it occurred in the Far East. On 30 September and 1 October, eight Tupolev Tu-22M *Backfire* supersonic bombers carried out simulated attacks on the US aircraft carriers *Enterprise* and *Midway* in the north Pacific. The *Backfires* approached to within 120 miles of the carrier task force and locked on with their AS-4 *Kitchen* anti-ship missiles before turning away and returning to their base at Aleksyevka (49 14N 140 11E). Although *Backfires* had been sighted before, this was the first time that such an attack profile had had been set up, and it demonstrated that the Tu-22M, first deployed in 1974, represented a substantial threat to western naval power. The *Backfire* was capable of multiple missions that encompassed nuclear strike, conventional strike, anti-shipping, mining and reconnaissance; some were later configured as ELINT aircraft, replacing the Tu-16 *Badger*.

In September 1983 a large multi-facet exercise was conducted with surface, subsurface, aircraft, merchant and fishing fleet participation. It was worldwide and demonstrated the Soviet ability to conduct and control major large-scale naval operations in all the major oceans at one time. This was the biggest observed co-ordination of merchant and fishing vessels to date. The exercise was designed to provide experience in carrying out tactical strike operations against a series of threats, in handling large resupply and amphibious convoys, and in conducting escort group operations in open-ocean ASW operations.

During *Springex 84*, which was held between 26 March and 21 April, the Northern Fleet conducted a large-scale deployment to the Norwegian Sea, with about half the Northern Fleet's surface combatants and a high proportion of the submarine order of battle participating. It was the largest exercise of its type yet seen. Two aggressor groups, consisting mainly of Krivak class ships simulating NATO forces, carried out an incursion into northern waters, one group deploying from the Northern Fleet and one from the Baltic. Defending forces included a large task force consisting of the new 25,000-ton cruiser *Kirov*, medium anti-surface-vessel destroyers of the Sovremenny class, anti-submarine destroyers of the Udaloy class, and older classes of warship. Air activity during the exercise was substantial, including attacks by *Backfires* against the Kirov group and air strikes directed against the Kola peninsula's bases.

The ability of the Russians to deploy so many warships and supporting units at one time and with speed came as a surprise to NATO. The lesson was clear: if the Soviet Navy could achieve similar surprise at the outset of a real conflict it would be able to secure the northern part of the Norwegian Sea and so prevent the deployment of NATO reinforcements to northern Norway in the event of a Soviet offensive. The exercise was repeated in July 1985, when at least 50 surface units, supported by submarines and aircraft, manoeuvred for three weeks in the Norwegian Sea while other smaller naval forces put to sea elsewhere around the periphery of the USSR.

No-one could have envisaged, at that time, that in just a few years the perceived threat from the East would have dwindled almost to nothing, and that the main threat to world security would come from elsewhere. But the quarter-century of Soviet naval expansion had convinced the NATO planners that constant surveillance of Soviet intentions in the maritime field was a principal key to survival.

19

Present and Future

AS LONG AS nations threaten war against one another, there will always be a need for air reconnaissance; and it would be an error to think that manned surveillance aircraft can ever be replaced fully by observation and intelligence-gathering satellites, even though these have been an enormous asset to defence intelligence agencies ever since the first American SAMOS photographic intelligence satellites were placed in orbit in the early 1960s.

In the 1982 Falklands War between Great Britain and Argentina, it was manned aircraft, rather than satellites, which provided essential reconnaissance. In April 1982, Victor K.2s of No. 57 Squadron RAF, operating from Wideawake airfield on Ascension Island, undertook sorties of 14 hours or more, carrying out maritime radar reconnaissance prior to the re-taking of South Georgia. Later, Nimrods pooled from Nos 120, 201 and 206 Squadrons carried out a similar task before the main landings on the Falkland Islands, flying sorties of over 19 hours' duration from Wideawake that took them to within 60 miles of the Argentine coast.

In the Gulf War, just under a decade later, satellites and manned aircraft combined to produce highly effective reconnaissance. No fewer than 14 US intelligence-gathering satellite systems were deployed in support of Operation *Desert Shield*, the build-up phase prior to the launching of the Coalition offensive, *Desert Storm*, against Iraq. Just a few years earlier, before the end of the Cold War, such a deployment would have been impossible, as it would have involved the diversion of reconnaissance systems from routine surveillance of the Soviet Union.

The satellite systems used in the Gulf fell into three broad categories: optical reconnaissance, radar surveillance and signals intelligence, the latter category being sub-divided into electronic intelligence (ELINT) and communications intelligence (COMINT). The most important system in the first category was the KH-11/KH-12 *Key Hole* optical imaging satellite, two of each type being deployed in support of the Gulf operations. Developed jointly by the US Air Force and the Central Intelligence Agency, the first *Key Hole* satellite was launched in December 1976 and the system has been constantly updated and refined since then. *Key Hole* is, in effect, a military version of the Hubble Space Telescope, with a length of 64 feet and a diameter of $6\frac{1}{2}$ feet. It can remain in orbit for two years, following an elliptical path varying between 185 and 275 miles above the earth. Data and pictures from its sensors are transmitted to ground stations in digital form, and in good conditions its high-resolution cameras can detect objects the size of a grapefruit on the ground. It is also equipped with infra-red cameras that can detect heat emissions from missiles, aircraft and vehicles.

In the second category, the principal radar reconnaissance satellite system was *Lacrosse*, which was first launched in 1988 and which follows a similar type of orbit to *Key Hole*. *Lacrosse* carries a synthetic aperture radar system which enables it to scan the earth's surface by day, night and in all weathers, even through clouds. The lens can resolve objects three feet across. The reflected radar waves are analysed by the satellite's on-board equipment, and the information passed to ground stations by relay satellites.

Two main satellite systems were used in the signals intelligence-gathering role. These were *Magnum* and *Chalet*, the former launched by the Space Shuttle and the latter by a Titan 34D booster. The task of both systems was to monitor 'walkie-talkie', telephone and radio, radar, microwave and telemetry transmissions from geostationary orbits 22,500 miles above the earth. The signals were 'dumped' to the Pine Gap receiving station in Australia, and then re-transmitted via communications satellites to other ground stations.

One vital function in the Gulf War was performed by another geostationary satellite system called DPS (Defence Programme Support) 14. Launched in November 1990, its task was to provide early warning of Iraqi missile launches. It was fitted with a powerful infra-red telescope, operating in two wavelengths to avoid laser jamming. The telescope detected rocket exhaust plumes against the Earth's background. During surveillance of Iraq, images were transmitted constantly to the USAF tracking station at Alice Springs and routed via several communications links to the Missile Early Warning Center at NORAD, Colorado; the information was also passed to ground terminals in Saudi Arabia, alerting Patriot SAM batteries to the threat of incoming *Scuds*.

While satellite reconnaissance information was essential to the building up of an overall strategic picture of events in the Gulf, however, the tactical control and direction of the war was the responsibility of two main airborne systems, the Boeing E-3 Sentry Airborne Warning and Control System (AWACS) and the Lockheed TR-1A battlefield surveillance aircraft.

The Boeing E-3, originally known as the EC-137, stemmed from a NATO requirement for an early warning aircraft equipped with radar systems capable of extending the low-altitude radar view of Warsaw Pact territory by as much as 150 miles, thereby filling the existing gaps in low-altitude coverage left by ground-based radars, and providing a major advance in early warning protection. The aircraft's role was summed up by General John S. Pustay, Director of the USAF AWACS Task Force, speaking in 1976, a year before the first E-3As entered USAF service:

'The E-3A would not only be able to track enemy formations as they approach the border; it would also make very difficult the deceptive forward assembly of large numbers of aircraft. Through routine surveillance...we could monitor typical aircraft activity patterns throughout East Germany and the western portions of Czechoslovakia and Poland. We could then determine changes in patterns which may be threatening – not only an obvious infusion of attack aircraft at forward bases, but more subtle activities such as the movement of support and transport aircraft out of the forward zone to clear ramp and hangar space to an unusual degree. Acting on such changes in pattern, or whenever our intelligence suggests a need for more concentrated surveillance, we could deploy more E-3As and fly continuous orbits to provide uninterrupted surveillance.'

A Boeing E-3 AWACS in NATO livery.

Although the perceived threat from the East has receded over the horizon, if not vanished entirely, the core of the E-3's role today remains the detection of an air threat. Its primary function in the Gulf War was to detect the movement of Iraqi aircraft and to direct Allied fighters to the point where a successful interception could be made. It has been used extensively for surveillance of the former Yugoslavia, providing intelligence of aircraft, helicopter and missile battery movements that might present a threat to UN peacekeeping forces.

At the heart of the E-3's systems is its Westinghouse surveillance radar, which can track targets more than 200 nautical miles away while the E-3 orbits at 30,000 feet. The 30-ft diameter radome turns at six revolutions per minute when the equipment is active, and has various operating modes depending on the task in hand. The standard E-3A's radar was later modified to track ships, and other modifications included the fitting of a faster central computer with expanded memory, together with improved communications equipment. This included the Joint Tactical Information Distribution System (JTIDS), which ensures an unbroken transmission of data if main communications links are disrupted.

The Gulf War also saw the first operational use of the Boeing E-8 JSTARS (Joint Surveillance Target Attack Radar System) aircraft. Developed from the Boeing 707 airliner, the E-8 carries very advanced surveillance systems to detect second-echelon ground concentrations deep behind enemy lines. The aircraft's computers then broadcast target information to both air and ground forces, directing in tactical strike aircraft, missile strikes or artillery as required. Other USAF stand-off electronic warfare aircraft deployed to the Gulf were the RC-135 and the EC-130H *Compass Call* communications jamming version of the Hercules.

The US Navy's principal electronic surveillance aircraft in the Gulf War, and the

The Grumman E-2 Hawkeye has been the 'eyes' of the US Navy since 1964.

mainstay of the USN's early warning capability for many years, was the Grumman E-2 Hawkeye, the prototype of which first flew on 20 October 1960. The first 20 E-2As were used for service evaluation and carrier trials, and the type was formally accepted into US Navy service in January 1964, when it began to equip Early Warning Squadron VAW-11 at San Diego. This unit went to sea with its Hawkeyes aboard the USS *Kitty Hawk* in 1966, by which time a second squadron, VAW-12, had also been formed. Sixty-two E-2As were built, including the prototypes, and construction ended early in 1967.

The E-2B, which flew in February 1969, had a number of refinements including an L-304 micro-electronic computer, and all operational E-2As were subsequently updated to E-2B standard. The early model Hawkeyes were equipped with the General Electric APS-96 search and tracking radar, which even in its original form was capable of automatic target detection and tracking over water. To achieve this, a technique called airborne moving target indication (AMTI) was introduced to suppress unwanted echoes from the sea. The APS-96 equipped E-2A and B were designed for 'blue water' operations far from land, but early operational experience – particularly in the Vietnam War – showed that the Hawkeye could be required to operate close to land and to detect targets against ground clutter. This posed problems for the APS-96, and in 1965 the US Navy began trials with a modified radar, the APS-111. Further trials and modifications to reject unwanted ground signals resulted in a new radar, the APS-120, which was capable of target detection and tracking over both sea and land. The system was fitted in a new model, the E-2C.

The latest version of the radar is the APS-145, which really gets to grips with the problems of ground clutter, using a technique called environmental processing to eliminate radar false alarms produced, say, by fast motorway traffic. The overland performance of the APS-145 is close to that of the E-3's surveillance radar and extends the Hawkeye's detection range to 350 miles.

A US Navy Hawkeye squadron usually comprises five aircraft, their task being to patrol a task force at a radius of about 200 nautical miles, their radar searching for hostile targets at all levels from the sea up to 100,000 feet. Standing off from a task force at a range of between 50 and 100 nm on the threat side, the Hawkeye can track up to 200 targets simultaneously, and provide automatic directions to defending Grumman F-14 Tomcat fighters via data link, assigning targets in order of priority. In war or a real threat situation, one Hawkeye would be airborne over the fleet 24 hours a day.

All kinds of jamming techniques were used in the Gulf War. Many were developed as the result of Vietnam experience, but others dated back to the Second World War. These included noise jamming, which is still one of the simplest methods of degrading radar performance. Radar signals use a lot of energy in the process of travelling to, and reflecting from, the target, so it is a relatively simple matter to drown them out with artificially created noise. Some noise jammers are set to operate on the single frequency used by the hostile radar, while others spread out their energy over a band of frequencies in the technique known as barrage jamming. Its disadvantage is that the jammer output is spread out along the spectrum instead of being concentrated on the actual operating frequency, so that in a 'one-against-one' engagement most of the energy is wasted. The other method, called spot jamming, involves knowing the exact enemy operating frequency before the start of a mission (which is where signals intelligence comes in) or alternatively using a receiver and signal processor to detect the signal, and then tuning the jammer to its frequency. Another well-used technique is swept-spot jamming, in which the jammer operating frequency scans through a band of enemy radar frequencies.

The most widely used ECM technique in the Gulf War was deception jamming, which provides hostile radar with false data. The technique involves receiving the signal from the radar, processing it in some way, then re-transmitting it in an attempt to persuade the radar to accept the spurious signal and derive false range and bearing information from it. The technique can have a disastrous effect on the automatic signal-processing circuitry in a radar, causing the antenna to lose its lock on the target. As soon as the target is re-acquired the ECM system promptly repeats the trick.

False target generation can be used to create artificial returns on the hostile radar screen, signals which maintain tracks, manoeuvre and behave in every way like genuine targets. Used ruthlessly, as they were in the Gulf War by the USAF's EF-111 Raven and the US Navy's EA-6B Prowler electronic warfare aircraft, such techniques can completely overload the radar display, filling the screen with so many false targets that they merge into a continuous signal and make it impossible for the enemy to implement any viable countermeasures.

Boeing B-52s were used in the Gulf War, armed with a very effective ECM fit. As a result of the B-52's vulnerability to SAM attack in the Vietnam War, an ECM modification programme called *Rivet Ace* was begun in 1974; at first, this involved incorporating updates into the B-52's existing ECM equipment (designated Phase VII update), but at a later date the entire ECM suite was revamped when the B-52 received a new Offensive Avionics System.

The Phase VII ECM equipment included the Westinghouse AN/ALQ-153 tail warning radar, also used in the F-15 and F-111, and the full Northrop AN/ALQ-155 ECM suite, which is based on broad-bandwidth receiving equipment, a signal processor and up to eight transmitters. The system also uses ALT-28 microwave

Boeing B-52G, 57-6476, of the 2nd Bombardment Wing, Barksdale AFB, showing nose blisters housing ALT-28 microwave transmitters. (A. A. B. Todd)

transmitters, mounted in blisters on either side of the B-52's nose under the cockpit, and the ALQ-117 *Pave Mint* defensive jamming system, the equipment for which is mounted in a tail extension. In addition to this electronic jamming equipment, all B-52Gs and Hs can carry up to 192 infrared countermeasures flares, carried on pylons between the engine installations on each wing.

The experience of Vietnam, however, had taught the Americans caution; the B-52s were not sent into action against enemy troop and vehicle concentrations until the threat of Iraq's Soviet-supplied surface-to-air missiles had been removed. The biggest threat to the high-level bombers came from the SA-6 *Gainful*, a fully mobile system deployed in rounds of three on a PT-76 chassis. A battery comprised four such launch vehicles, with target data supplied by a *Straight Flush* radar vehicle. Israeli combat aircraft suffered heavy losses from the SA-6 during the Yom Kippur War of 1973.

The SA-6, however, was vulnerable in one respect: all four launch vehicles could be rendered ineffective if the *Straight Flush* vehicle was destroyed, and this was achieved with great efficiency in the Gulf War by Allied 'Wild Weasel' aircraft using anti-radar missiles.

Allied knowledge of the limitations of the SA-6, and of other Russian defensive systems at Iraq's disposal, was the result of constant eavesdropping on the Soviet Union by NATO strategic reconnaissance aircraft during the long years of the Cold War.

It was a library of knowledge that made swift victory possible, with minimum Coalition casualties.

The Lockheed EC-130A Compass Call *electronic jamming version of the Hercules.* (Colin Lambert)

Strategic air reconnaissance continues to be one of the greatest assets to world stability. U-2s and TR-1s continue to ply their trade around the globe, maintaining surveillance of potential trouble-spots and monitoring UN peace-keeping activities. Their successors, extremely long range aircraft using stealth technology to the fullest advantage, are on the drawing boards and in some cases have already flown in prototype form. It will be very hard, in the world of the 21st century, for a totalitarian state to make an aggressive move undetected, or to produce weapons of mass destruction in secrecy.

Index